The
MLM
ROAD MAP

Also by

Ray H. Duncan

The MLM BINARY PLAN

The
MLM
ROAD MAP

A Step-By-Step System Of Building A Network Marketing DOWNLINE

By
Ray H. Duncan

Double Diamond Publishing
New Orleans, LA 70124

Library of Congress Catalog-in-Publication Data
Duncan, Ray H.
The MLM ROAD MAP : A Step-by-Step System of Building a Network Marketing Downline / by Ray H. Duncan.
    p.   cm.
    Includes Index
1st Edition
    ISBN 1-929746-00-8
1. Road Map 2. Network Marketing 3. MLM
Library of Congress Catalog Card Number: 99-091138

Contents

"Far better it is to dare mighty things, to win glorious triumphs, even though checkered by failure, than to take rank with those poor spirits who neither enjoy much nor suffer much, because they live in the gray twilight that knows not victory nor defeat."

Teddy Roosevelt

ACKNOWLEDGMENTS

This book is dedicated to my parents Roy and Joy Duncan, whose support has been my inspiration throughout the years. I also dedicate this work to my wife Beth, who has shared my faith in the American free enterprise system, to my son Hunter, and to my daughters Catherine and Frances.

I would like to thank the following for their influence and help: Peter and Andrew Spary, MultiSoft Corporation, Cape Coral, Florida; Roger G. Harvey, McComb, Mississippi; Bill Worden, New Orleans, Louisiana; Jon Steenbakker, Ft. Lauderdale, FL; Rich Rowland, Kansas City, Missouri; Tom Schreiter, Houston, Texas; Dale Maloney, Eau Claire, Wisconsin; Rick Lawrence, Garland, Texas; Ben Mayberry, Tulsa, Oklahoma; Randy Ward, Broken Arrow, Oklahoma; Ron Warren, Steele, Alabama; Dan Fagan, St. Louis, Missouri; George Strahan, McCall Creek, Mississippi; Rodney Fleetwood, New Orleans, Louisiana; Johnny Johnson, Arlington Plantation, Franklin, Louisiana; Corky Sadler, San Antonio, Texas; J.T. Rainer, Phoenix, AZ; and the hundreds of people that I have met in the industry whose conversation or enthusiasm has helped shape my network marketing techniques.

I would also like to thank those individuals that have formed network marketing companies and offer an alternative method of earning income that does not limit the potential of those who accept the challenge.

Ray H. Duncan, 1999

Foreword

In our business, we meet people every day that have the magical gift of leadership. The qualities they possess and the ways they use them make them what they are -- great people.

And then, we meet people like Ray Duncan, who looks for and helps others to develop the greatness within them. His belief in people combined with his systemized approach to building a network marketing sales organization is his passion.

As a college graduate with a masters in business administration, I have always felt that education is paramount to success and especially so in network marketing. The few who possess the necessary skills in the beginning are lucky; the many that must develop those skills are fortunate that this book has been published. Now, everyone can learn these basics that will help them on their journey.

This is a book that teaches Network Marketing basics and a step-by-step system of downline development that will help you to build a strong and stable foundation to your organization. As a full-time network marketer for over fifteen years, I have had the opportunity to develop many successful organizations with this system, organizations that produced a lifestyle for me that only corporate executives enjoy - - and more!

I feel extremely fortunate for the opportunity to work with Ray on the development of this book, and I know that by following this system you will be headed in the right direction for financial independence.

Bill Worden, MBA
Lifetime Entrepreneur, New Orleans, Louisiana

*"The secret of finding success is not to do what you like to do,
but to learn to like what you have to do."*

CHAPTER 1

INTRODUCTION TO NETWORK MARKETING

You have entered a very exciting and financially rewarding occupation, Network Marketing. You will be developing a sales organization of your own called a "downline." Your financial gain will reflect the amount of work you put into your downline. This book's system is designed to streamline your efforts while giving you some proven directions on where to start and what to do after you are started. I am going to repeat some statements again and again because I want them to be indelibly stamped in your memory.

Network Marketing, often referred to as Multilevel Marketing, is basically direct sales. A corporation enlists Independent Marketing Representatives to sell its products to the consumer. The marketing dollars are paid directly to the sales force. There are no jobbers, wholesalers, distributors, or warehouses with which they have to share the profit. This form of marketing allows Independent Marketing Representatives to create a downline sales organization of their own. You, as an Independent Marketing Representative, will pay for all shipping and promotional materials such as products, sales aids, order forms, etc. The percentage of the marketing dollar is the same; it is just distributed in commissions and bonuses directly to your downline. In traditional product marketing, roughly one half of every retail dollar goes to the manufacturers (1/4 cost, 1/4 profit); the other half is distributed to jobbers, wholesalers, and retailers. Network marketing pays the same percentage to the manufacturers, and the marketing half is paid to the network of distributors (you and your downline). Thus, your downline performs the role of jobber, wholesaler, and distributor and shares these profits (retail markup, commissions, and bonuses).

True network marketing, or multilevel compensation, is based on sales volume. The higher your downline sales volume is, the higher your commissions are. Some people unknowingly refer to network marketing as pyramiding. It is NOT a pyramid system! The main difference lies in the basis of compensation. Pyramid schemes are centered on payment for recruiting, NOT SALES! Also, pyramid schemes have room for only one person at the highest pay level. True network marketing offers each person the same opportunity.

It's exciting to think of just starting out in network marketing! You have so many exciting times ahead of you in this field. You have, or are about to purchase, an Independent Distributor's Kit from the company. Study all of the printed material and learn the rules and regulations set forth by the company. Follow the company's guidelines to success. Ask your upline or write the company for information about any area that is unclear.

Success is gained through one word: COMMITMENT. You must have the commitment to your future, your product, and your organization to be successful. Commitment means giving what it takes - - WHAT-EVER IT TAKES. If you need to learn to sell, then commitment will demand that you study sales. This applies to anything you need to do to become successful. You might as well sit down right now and find out if you have the commitment to become successful. If you do not already have it, then are you willing to make that pledge in order to become successful? Your commitment and the commitment of each person you sponsor should be a ONE-YEAR dedication.

You are starting on a journey of success. The next few months will not only be a wonderful learning experience, but also a start toward financial security. Since your basic function is to sell products and sponsor new distributors, you need to develop professional skills in both areas.

FIRST IMPRESSIONS, those made within the first few seconds of meeting, are lasting ones. It is imperative for you to create the best first impression you can on all prospects you meet. Appearance, Professionalism, Product Knowledge, Sales Presentation, Downline Development, Service, Training, Follow-Up, Motivation, & Communication are important keys to success in this industry. These topics are discussed in the following pages.

APPEARANCE is possibly the most influential factor in network marketing. Our profession projects success; therefore, we should always strive to make ourselves appear successful. You must project a professional sales appearance to support your program. Prospects make a judgment on you immediately when you start your introduction. Appearance is the first thing they notice; it will weigh heavily on their opinion of you, your company, and your products. Always present a clean, well-groomed, and neatly dressed image when calling on clients; it makes a difference. I am not implying that men have to wear a three-piece suit or have a military haircut, or that women must be dressed

in business attire. I do recommend that you take care to dress properly for the occasion. Since most of your contacts will be casual, you will usually wear casual type clothes. The distributors you sponsor into the sales program will learn from you and will follow your example. Three words can best describe the appearance you need to develop: DRESS FOR SUCCESS.

PROFESSIONALISM is a topic on which volumes could be written, but the key here is to remember that you are representing a major company, its products, and everyone else that derives income from it. This could be a lot of people, so strive to adhere to the professional standards of our industry. Remember to maintain a proper appearance and to give careful attention to your presentations. I know a distributor who carries his products, samples, and collateral materials to sales calls in an old cardboard box yet makes as professional a presentation as you will ever see. On the other hand, I have known others who were equipped with the finest leather cases, but were completely unorganized and ineffective. You must be well prepared and organized in order to make a professional presentation. I prefer to carry applications, printed materials, and order forms in a briefcase and use a salesman's sample bag for my products. This gives me a chance to arrange things of a kind together and make an orderly presentation, thereby strengthening my credibility and promoting a better understanding on the part of my prospect.

PRODUCT KNOWLEDGE is another important "must" for every salesperson. You simply cannot sell anything unless you have thorough knowledge of it. Also, knowledge about the company you are representing is included here. Would you buy a product from a sales representative that could not explain about the company or did not know anything about the product? Of course you would not, and neither would I! You do not have to be an expert, either. Just equip yourself with a working knowledge of the products you represent, and you will do fine.

Your work is cut out for you. Learn about the company and the product so you can give a brief but complete description of both. Become a "Product of the Product" and use the products yourself. The best way of knowing and feeling the result of your product or service is to use it. By doing so, you will be able to talk to others with knowledge and self-confidence.

SALES PRESENTATION is equally important in sales of any product line. Your presentation should be brief, culminating with the prospect's purchasing one or more of your products and understanding the opportunity your company offers. To achieve these results, you must have knowledge of both the products and the company's opportunity.

You can visit with other distributors in your area at your next meeting and find out what presentations are bringing them success. Brainstorming with other distributors is very rewarding and can be loads of fun. What is wrong with having fun with your career? Nothing; it makes you feel better, and you will never think of it as a job. Your local bookstore and library have books on sales techniques. You can learn much from these references, and I suggest you do so. Listen to other sales representatives give their presentations. If they are successful, then you will learn something from them. And, by all means, listen to your upline sponsor! Remember that your sponsor knows much more than you about the products and opportunity.

DOWNLINE DEVELOPMENT involves a system of creating and building a growing sales organization. There is a step-by-step blueprint to follow, which we call a "Road Map." The specifics of this Road Map comprise the heart of this book. You will learn each step as you read along and be able to determine for yourself the techniques of successful downline development.

SERVICE is another key that signifies professionalism. Your customers will expect prompt and efficient service from you on all orders. Do not let them down - - take care of the hand that feeds you! Remember that bad service will hurt your downline and adversely affect your income as well as reflect on the company, its products, and its representatives. Service is equally important to your downline. You are expected to give members of your downline top-notch service and by setting this example, you will be training without effort.

TRAINING is paramount and should be ongoing. You must train members of your downline to follow in your footsteps and create their own downlines, thus duplicating your efforts. You can train by example. By setting an example for others to follow, you are making your job as a teacher easier. You will find that most of your downline members will want to emulate you and by setting the right example for them to follow, you are moving closer to success.

You need to hold scheduled training meetings apart from opportunity meetings to improve the success of your downline. These meetings should offer training in sales, product knowledge, downline development, and company policy. You, as the leader of your downline, must keep up to date with your company in order to pass new information along to your downline members.

Sales training should cover all aspects of a sale, including initial contact, dialogue, follow-up, and proper handling of paper work. Companies are constantly expanding their product lines and improving their product literature and sales aids. It is your responsibility, as a leader, to pass this information on to your downline. It is impossible for you, as head of a large organization, to inform all of your downline, so you must pick leaders from your group and teach them to train their people. Such practice is all part of networking. This building system will make you and your organization more successful, thus increasing your profits.

One aspect of training should always be product presentation. It is too easy for members of your downline to become excessively enthusiastic about the company's products. Statements referring to results of product use can get out of hand when trying to make a sale or in sponsoring. You must firmly control, through training, what is being said about product results and income claims. Your training program should cover both recruitment and downline development. Helping your people develop their organizations will strengthen your overall organization.

FOLLOW-UP is one of the most important aspects of network marketing. When you meet a prospect and give him or her a sample, you must actively follow-up this lead in order to develop that person into a customer or distributor. Always try to find out exactly when the best time is to reach your prospect by phone. The follow-up should be soon after the first introduction, and many times you must re-establish yourself with the prospect. Follow-up should continue as long as your distributors are active in your program and, in many instances, should continue even after they have left the program. Personal contact, or follow-up, is a basic communication practice that must be utilized with every prospect, distributor, customer, and ex-customer.

EXAMPLE:

"Well, what do you like best about XYZ MLM Company?" OR
"What did you like best about our XYZ Widget product?"

Many network marketers never ask the prospect what they think, but I believe that it is vitally important to do so. It lets you know right up front what situation you are dealing with. Some call it "THE MIL-LION DOLLAR QUESTION," and it may be! If the prospect does not like the product you are offering, you simply do not have anything else to discuss. You may gain a few referrals by asking if he/she knows anyone else who might like to try a sample or make extra money by becoming a distributor. However, if your prospect just does not like your product, you may as well go on to someone else.

Follow-up is extremely important when it comes to answering your advertising prospects. If you are using a phone recorder or voice mail system, you will be returning phone calls. It will be important to follow-up these inquiries soon after they initiated the call to you. You will need to make notes on each prospect so you will know something about the types of people that your advertising is attracting. The notes you take will influence future follow-ups. You may have to follow-up with your prospects several times during the period they are considering your opportunity. Be patient, and take notes regarding what they say about themselves.

Your success in network marketing will depend greatly on the follow-up you do with your prospects and distributors. One method of organizing your schedule to be sure you follow-up on time is to keep a daily journal. This will help you organize your time and keep notes on your call backs. Remember, follow-up all visits and samples with a phone call - - within 24 hours if possible.

Once, I rented a booth at a trade show and enlisted other members of my downline to work and share responsibilities of the booth. We passed out a few thousand samples of our company's great weight loss herb and thought we were really going great guns. Then we discovered that we could have done much better if we had asked each prospect for his/her phone number. This would have allowed my group to follow-up with everyone we gave a sample to.

MOTIVATION and COMMUNICATION. To achieve success in network marketing, you must become proficient in motivating members of your downline. The best way to do this is to find their "hot button." You must find out just what it is that they want. This is not as easy as it sounds, because most people just do not know what they want. You must learn to help them find what it is that they really desire.

EXAMPLE*: "Sam, if you made the decision right now to join me and start your own XYZ business, what is it exactly that you would want or expect from it?"*

SAM: *"I would like to be financially free."*

YOU*: "Sam, financially free can mean a lot of different things. Can you put it into hard dollars? Just how much do you need to earn each month to allow you to feel financially free?"*

SAM: *"Well, if you put it that way, I need to make at least $10,000 per month."*

YOU: *"Fine, I thought you had a figure we could work with. Now, how much are you making with your present job?"*

SAM: *"I earn $4,200 per month at my present job."*

YOU: *"So you are telling me that you want to make $5,800 ."*

SAM: *"That's right."*

YOU: *"Sam, If I commit to helping you earn this much money each*

18

month from XYZ, would you commit yourself to an Action Plan?"

SAM: "Yes I would, but what do I have to do?"

YOU: "I want you to follow a step-by-step system and commit four to eight hours a week. This will include attending meetings, listening to conference training calls, and setting presentations to prospects."

SAM: "If you will help me, I will do what you ask."

YOU: "Fine, now let's complete the paperwork and get you started."

You have successfully helped Sam to find out his true wants and turn them into a goal. You have received a commitment from him to do whatever it takes to achieve this goal. Now you must help design an action plan that will allow Sam to focus on and reach his goal of earning $5,800 per month from his new XYZ business.

EXAMPLE:

YOU: "You will need to build an organization of distributors to earn $5,800 per month. First, you will need to build your prospect list and start setting appointments. I will go with you and make the presentations for you and help sponsor your first two distributors. Then, after doing the same for these two distributors, we will sponsor you a third distributor." SHOW the Building System!

SAM: "But how long will it take? I want this as fast as possible!"

YOU: "I cannot answer that question for you, but how much longer will *it take for you to get raises totaling $5,800 per month in your present job?"*

SAM: *"NEVER."*

YOU: *"That's the reason you need to commit yourself to Network Marketing! If you can introduce me to people you know, starting tomorrow, I will help you sponsor your first two distributors and teach you how to sponsor also. Could you do that?"*

SAM: *"Yes, I could do that."*

YOU: *"If these people realize the opportunity and sponsor into the program, you will have your first two distributors to work with. Now, I want you to review the products and opportunity and study the Policies and Procedures of the company over the next 24 hours. I also want you to use this Prospect Generator and make a list of people we can make presentations to or invite to a group overview. I have a system I want you to use to start your business; here is the first page. I will call you tomorrow, and we will make presentations to some of the people on your list. I want you to call your list and schedule two appointments for us each day next week. I want to help you reach the Executive position as fast as I can."*

Now, you should have John convinced that if he allows himself enough time, he will succeed. Some people need to understand this principle before they can proceed with network marketing. Others must see the power of duplication before they will commit to giving up some of their time and energy for an opportunity. You have also committed your own time to make presentations with him.

Jan	Feb	Mar	Apr	May	Jun	Jul	Aug	Sep	Oct	Nov	Dec	TOTAL
2	4	8	16	32	64	128	256	512	1024	2048	4096	**8190**

THE TIMELINE

The above is a "TIMELINE." If you started your network business in January by sponsoring just 2 people, you would have 2 under Jan. If you worked with these two people for each to sponsor 2 people, you would have 4 under FEB and a total of 6 people in your sales group. Now, if you worked with your first two people to help their two people sponsor 2 each, you would have 8 under MAR and a total of 14 in your sales organization. Then, if you helped these 8 each sponsor 2, you would have 16 under APRIL and a total of 30 in your sales organization.

See how you can grow if everyone made just 2 sales? By the end of ONE calendar year, you could have a total of 8,190 people in your sales organization. Now use this to show why your prospect or new distributor should commit to ONE YEAR!

The TIMELINE shows the power of building an organization of duplication! With proper training in presenting your program plus help from upline members, the TIMELINE is a great achievable goal, exemplifying the potential of the duplication principle.

THREE-WAY TO SUCCESS

There is an old saying that everyone has heard: "What you don't know won't hurt you." In network marketing it is the exact opposite: "What you don't know will definitely hurt you," at least in sponsoring new distributors. When you are making a presentation, you must know what to say and when to say it. This is the reason that you must NEVER approach prospects by yourself. Remember, "ON THE PHONE, NEVER ALONE" and "NEVER APPROACH WITHOUT A COACH." You must let your sponsor or an upline member make the presentations, either in person or on a three-way phone call. Other than making personal presentations with your sponsor, the three-way phone call to a prospect is the best method of sponsoring new distributors.

If you do not have three-way calling on the telephone you use, call your service provider immediately and request three-way calling. It will only cost a few dollars each month and will be the best investment in your future that you will ever make.

For proper use of three-way calling, you should print a list of names and phone numbers of your upline that you will be using and keep it close to your telephone. Your sponsor and other qualified upline members will become your three-way calling list. You should contact these people and find out what times they will be available for three-way calling to your prospects and how they recommend handling the calls.

There are several methods of conducting three-way phone presentations, but first you need to qualify your prospect. The following represents two distinct methods of three-way phone presentations:

1. The "Add-On Phone Partner." Call your prospect and set up for the presentation.

YOU: *"Hello John, this is Sam. Are you open to an opportunity today?"*

JOHN: *"Well, I guess so."*

YOU: *"Great! John, I think I have found the perfect opportunity, and I would like to put Jim Smith on the phone for just a few minutes so he can explain it to you."*

Now, this is where you connect to Jim Smith. After you make the introduction, let Jim Smith do his job and make the presentation to John.

The credibility of a third party is always strong. In the above example, you qualified your prospect for the presentation by asking him if he were open for an opportunity. Then when you received a positive answer, you brought your upline member Jim Smith on the call to make the presentation. Although your prospect does not know Jim Smith, he will consider him to be more of an expert than you. This is the power of the third party presentation.

2. The "Carry-On Phone Presentation." In this method, you will call your three-way partner and have him/ her on the line with you when you are calling prospects. The rest is simple: just introduce your prospect to your three-way partner and listen.

YOU: *"Hello John, This is Sam. Are you open for an opportunity?"*

JOHN: *"Yes, I have a few minutes."*

YOU: *"I have Jim Smith on the phone with me. Jim is one of the area's top producers, and I would like for him to tell you what we are doing."*

Now your job is finished; just let Jim do his job and make the phone presentation. You will be learning Jim's presentation to your prospects and as you build your organization, you will eventually assume his role with your distributors.

When the conversation is over, always check the line to make sure your party was disconnected. There have been many mistakes made even by professional network marketers because they did not check to see if the line cleared.

THIRD PARTY PRESENTATIONS

Obviously, network marketing downlines are not developed from three-way phone calls alone. Even with the best phone presentations, most prospects will need further follow-up and confirmation. Perhaps the strongest closing presentations are the ones done in person. These can be done in the home or across the table in a restaurant. You should set appointments with your prospects and allow a strong upline member to accompany you and actually make the presentation. This is the ultimate method of sponsoring and building a network marketing downline. It is the system that has built large groups in this industry and will continue to be the most universal method of sponsoring. The use of a third party to make the presentation is essential and adds the necessary credibility. Your prospects will be far more apt to join your organization if they know that they can rely on strong upline support with sponsoring.

The building system in this book centers on third party presentations. No matter how strong your prospecting tools are, every prospect will need to be closed. Third party closing presentations will accomplish more than any other method.

When you graduate and become your distributors' three-way mentor, you will need to develop your own presentation to deliver. Listen to each presentation made by your third party partner and learn the strong points he/she uses. Adopt the best from these presentations into your own.

The use of three-way phone presentations and third party personal presentations is the process that will certainly help you succeed in network marketing.

CALL LOG

Organization is very important to the success of any recruiting campaign. You should create a call log and record each outbound call you make, as well as all inbound calls. The call log should have space for the prospect's name, phone number, and several lines of notes. With a call log, you can have this information available at your fingertips any time. You will find it invaluable, as it will provide a record of calls to and from each prospect or new recruit. You will be well-organized when you place your follow-up calls and will have total recall on past conversations.

You must create a Prospect Evaluator to record information about each prospect. It will become useful on follow-up calls and will greatly influence your degree of success in both sponsoring and working with prospects.

The following information should be gathered and listed on the Prospect Evaluator:

1. Name, address, city, state, zip, home phone, work phone, fax number, and e-mail address.
2. Marital status, spouse's name (if any), children (names and ages, if any).
3. Primary occupation, spouse's occupation.
4. Past MLM or Network Marketing experience.
5. Present MLM or Network Marketing company(s).
6. Desire level, commitment level.
7. Hobbies, outside activities, church affiliation.
8. Goals, hot button, time limit.

By asking questions and completing the evaluation sheet, you are not only gathering important information about your prospect, but you are also showing an interest in this person other than just sponsoring someone into your business. At least, that is how your line of questions will be perceived. Now when you do follow-up, you will know the spouse's name if he/she should answer the phone and can show interest by inquiring about children, job, etc. These icebreakers can really make a difference in recruiting results.

Keeping a call log with notes is the best way to become organized. Organization is a large factor of success.

CHAPTER 2
Tools of the Trade

Assembling the tools necessary to conduct business in a professional manner is an important step toward success. You should look
through the manual, price lists, or other literature your company
included in the start-up manual and find the tools available to you for
working your business. These include:

1. Brochures on your company or products.
2. Opportunity video and audio cassettes.
3. Business card order form.

You will need to have an ample supply of brochures . The worst thing
you can do is fail to have them when making presentations. Never
rely on your sponsor to furnish everything. This is your business,
and you are the responsible party. Be prepared!

If your company has video or audio cassette tapes that you can use for recruiting and sponsoring, carry a few with you at all times. Many companies produce recruiting video and audio tapes, and they are great tools you can use to build your business. You can combine the power of these tapes into your advertising:

This will pass the cost of the prospecting tools to your prospects and will screen them for you. Inside the package you should place a note instructing the prospect to review the material and share with a friend. This way, you will reach more than the one prospect with each mailing.

BUSINESS CARDS

Your business card is your "calling card." It is often the silent salesman that keeps your name and phone number with a prospect. Since your business card represents you and your opportunity long after the initial contact with your prospect, it is very important for you to have a professional business card. It should be attractive, appealing, easy to read, and contain a reminder of exactly what you do. Your prospect may have a stack of cards, and you and your opportunity could easily get lost and in the trash can unless the prospect can identify you with your product or opportunity.

If your company does not offer professional business cards that identify you with your specific opportunity or product, you will have to design your own. You may even wish to search for a graphic designer to design your business card. Whatever the cost might be, it will be a good investment. You may wish to have the graphic designer create stationary and envelopes that match the theme of your business card.

The "PnW" stands for Professional Network Marketer. Often titles behind your name will add to the importance of your card, especially if they keep it so they can ask you what "PnW" stands for.

This is YOUR "calling card," and it is an extension of you. It will be representing you when you are not around, so make sure that it represents you in the manner you wish! Your business card is like a billboard advertisement; it will sell for you when you are not around. It may be passed to different people who have not met you and will serve as a reminder to others of who you are and what you do.

WHEN TO PRESENT

There are such things as business card etiquette and business card psychology. The rule of professional etiquette is to hand your card out ONLY AFTER rapport has been established during conversation. Your business card will have much more effect on others when it is NOT FORCED. Proper timing at the end of a conversation is the rule.

Business card psychology can take on many different aspects. For example, Dale Maloney in his tape series, "Secrets of Multi-Level Marketing," teaches punching a hole in your business card to make it different from other people's cards. A philosophy of this technique is that people will keep the card, intending to ask what the hole is for. Another technique is to make a note on the back of the card when you hand it out. Your prospect will be reminded of the conversation by looking at the note you wrote. Giving a business card at the end of a conversation also serves to break down your prospect's resistance in giving his/her name and phone number.

Always carry more business cards than you think you will need and have them readily accessible. The worst thing you can do when presenting a business card is to fumble around looking for a card to hand out.

A good business card is the most economical tool you will ever use. Make sure you have a GREAT card, that you have an ample supply in an easily accessible location, and that you present it at the proper time.

CHAPTER 3

GETTING STARTED

After receiving your distributor kit and initial product order, you should schedule some time with your sponsor and have him/her explain anything you do not understand.

Your sponsor will appreciate your desire to get started on your journey and will help with your action plan and any questions you might have at this time. You will become a sponsor of others soon, so you should provide your time to those you sponsor. Work out a schedule with your sponsor and get your prospect list completed. No matter how you feel about certain people, you should place them on your list and make an attempt with them.

Getting started in any business is exciting, but in a network marketing opportunity, you will meet other distributors with the same mission as you, to become more financially stable through your own network business. Perhaps the very first thing you must do is to find out exactly what you want from this opportunity. Is it a certain amount of money, a new car, home, or a combination of several things? You must have answered this question to yourself before you can ask it of others.

Secondly, you should ask yourself, realistically, "When do I want this?" The answer to this question will determine how much time you should devote to your new business on a Daily, Weekly, and Monthly basis. You must make the personal commitment to do "Whatever it Takes" to accomplish your goals. With this type of commitment, you should be able to fulfill your goals within the time frame you set for yourself.

No matter which company you choose to work with, you are in business to sell products or services through a network of independent distributors. While high volumes of retail sales are profitable for you and the company, they are also profitable for those in your upline commission structure. Long-term financial rewards do not come from high retail volumes on your part. They are generated by a downline of your own distributors, selling the product and building downlines of their own. You must concentrate on becoming a leader of people and a teacher or trainer of your new profession. If you have a knack for selling your products, do not stop selling, but also teach this knack to members of your downline.

Now is the time to define the steps you must take to reach your goals. Write them down in a notebook, and let them become an action plan to help you ROAD MAP your success. You may want to seek the advice of a successful distributor in your upline when defining these steps. Basically, you will need an understanding of the compensation plan and the structure of distributors necessary to reach your goals. By following the building system as explained in this book, you will develop width and depth proportionally, and each leg will grow stronger every month. This system builds leaders.

You can separate the different steps of your action plan down to a Daily, Weekly, and Monthly system that will allow you to plot your successes or failures easily. If things are moving more slowly than your plan calls for, you must determine the reasons and make the necessary changes, either to your time schedule or to your own performance. Work with your sponsor to define the steps to success in your particular company. Ask your upline sponsor to assist you in defining your action plan, and ask for help in completing your goal sheets (building system).

DETERMINING YOUR ACTION PLAN

WEEKLY

1. Schedule one evening a week for a training meeting with your distributors.

2. Share the product and opportunity with someone each day and schedule a presentation (2 to 10 minutes) for you and your sponsor with this person.

3. Call all of your first level distributors each week to check on their progress and to determine what kind of help they need.

4. Allow time each day to help your distributors make presentations to their prospects.

5. Schedule time each week to find and interview new prospects for your first level (personally sponsored), and work with members of your downline that need help.

Your getting started actions should include:

1. Build your prospect list.
2. Study all company literature and material.
3.. Contact and schedule presentations with prospects from your list at prearranged meeting times with your sponsor.
4.. Obtain a working knowledge of your product and opportunity.

THE SHORT-TERM GOALS are perhaps the best ways of building your business, for often they are a lot easier to accomplish than shooting for the moon. The building system is the per-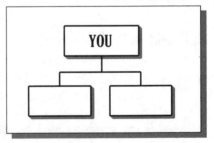fect set of short-term goals. Each step is a short-term goal. Work this system and use each step as a goal sheet. After receiving your distributor kit and initial product order, you should schedule some time with your sponsor to explain anything you do not understand.

Your sponsor will appreciate your desire to get started on your journey and will help you with your action plan and answer any questions you might have. You will become a sponsor of others soon, so you should provide your time likewise to those you sponsor. Work out a schedule with your sponsor and get your prospect list completed. No matter how you feel about certain people, you should place them on your list and schedule a presentation.

Your getting started list should include:

1. Distributor kit & manual
2. Initial supply of products
3. Application forms
4. Order forms
5. Product/Services brochures and promotional aids
6. Business cards
7. Prospect list with 100 names (created by you)
8. Action plan meeting with your sponsor (schedule presentations with prospects)

PROSPECT GENERATOR

A good definition of Success is "Where Preparedness meets Opportunity." Not that all successful people are always prepared for the opportunity at hand, but it helps. Your best method for building a super group of network marketers is to search out and recruit people who have a POSITIVE ATTITUDE - - those who are already respected and have the DESIRE to succeed. Ambitious people are all around us; we just have to learn to recognize them.

Generally, the more successful a person is already, the quicker he/she is to see the tremendous opportunity. Remember that you have something of immense value to them. Do not ever sell yourself short! Most will thank you the rest of their lives. You are offering the opportunity for financial freedom and the realization of their dreams. This is the chance and training for them to become successful!

WHEN BUILDING YOUR LIST, CONSIDER THE FOLLOWING:

- Friends
- Neighbors
- Relatives
- Church Members
- Fellow Employees
- Past Associates
- Club Members

- Christmas List
- Schoolmates
- People you respect
- People who have prospected you
- Anyone with entrepreneurial spirit

Begin calling your list with your sponsor at first and on your own when you feel confident. Learn company and product knowledge, attend all opportunity and training meetings, and listen in to the training calls. Become a "Product of the Product." Try a different product each month until you have used each product your company offers. Teach your distributors to do the same. Remember, as a network marketer, you are not allowed to say what the product has done for others, but you CAN SAY what it has done for YOU! Unless you use what you sell, you can not give a personal testimonial.

Do Not Pre-judge Your prospects!

WHO DO YOU KNOW?

Everyone you know or come in contact with has needs, just like yourself. To get started building your list, first write down all of the people you know in the entire world. Then, ask yourself who you know - - that:

- Is active in a church
- People always seem to like
- Is a professional
- Is in clubs, various groups
- Is in a teaching profession
- Deals with the public
- Is looking for something better out of life
- Is the leader of the group
- Has children in upper schools or college
- Is in a no-where job

- Lives next door
- Is my barber/hairdresser
- Teaches our children
- Was my best man
- Was our maid of honor
- Is a wedding photographer
- Is a fellow worker
- Is a hunting/fishing buddy
- Is baby sitter's parent
- Is an Army/Navy buddy
- Is a Real Estate Agent
- Is a bowling team member
- Is a PTA leader

START YOUR LIST

Sit down with no interruptions and start listing everyone you know. Remember not to pre-judge anyone. Work on your list each day. Always carry a note pad with you and write down names as they come to you. Transfer these names to your list as soon as you can. This list will be the starting point for your organization. You and your sponsor will make presentations to everyone on this list.

WORK AT A COMFORTABLE PACE AND LIST EVERYONE YOU PERSONALLY KNOW WHO MIGHT BE A PROSPECT FOR YOUR BUSINESS.

People I Know: **Date:** _____

_____

_____

_____

_____

_____

_____

_____

_____

_____

_____

_____

_____

_____

_____

_____

_____

_____

_____

_____

_____

_____

_____

_____

CHAPTER 4

RECRUITING PROSPECTS

To become successful in network marketing, we have learned that we need to build a downline. We must also train every member of our downline to duplicate our efforts and build a downline of their own. In theory, a certain number of these distributors will fall within our residual percentage levels, and we will earn from their efforts. Good network marketing teachers are rewarded for their efforts. In order to build a downline, we must find other people interested in becoming either a wholesale customer or a distributor. For now, we will concentrate on the potential distributor and call this person a "prospect." Everyone knows a certain number of people. Do you know twenty, forty, or a hundred people? These can be your start. List your prospects by simply writing their names down on a piece of paper. Your memory will develop as time goes on, and you will remember a name or two periodically that you failed to list. Just keep adding these names to your list and you will have a good start.

There are two markets you will reach with your new business: the WARM Market and the COLD Market. The WARM Market consists of family and friends, people you work with, or people you know. These people will be the first you should approach with your product and presentation. You will most certainly have a lot more credibility with them than with total strangers.

The "COLD Market List" is composed of people that you do not know yet, but will. The attendant at the gas station, the clerk at the store, the receptionist at the dentist's office are all prospects. You will, depending on your first impression and product and opportunity presentation, develop a certain amount of credibility with these "strangers." They do not know you well and are relying on the impression you initially make on them.

Successful network marketers all use the "Three-Foot Rule." Anyone that comes within three feet of you should hear about the product and the opportunity. By adhering to the Three-Foot Rule, you will constantly build your COLD Market List. Carry business cards with you at all times, as well as an assortment of products. This will allow you to do a Three-Foot at any time and any place. You should always ask for the person's name, address, and telephone number. A business card case that has a small note pad attached can be purchased at an office supply store and is ideal for writing down this information. It gives you a professional marketing tool for only a few dollars. There are several prospecting aids that can be used to cold recruit people you casually come in contact with. They are listed throughout this book.

EXAMPLE: *"Let me share a little booklet that has helped my family with our financial situation. Read it tonight, and I will pick it up from you tomorrow. My business card is in the back; may I have your phone number?"*

WARM MARKET LIST

You should divide this initial list into family, friends, and business contacts or fellow workers. Start off working with a few of each, and you will be surprised at the results. The people you know best may probably be reached by phone.

Organize your prospect list and set yourself a goal, let's say five calls per day. If you maintain five calls per day, you will have a respectable downline and volume in just a few months.

Other people you know can be contacted by phone or in person. Personal contacts are probably better, as you can directly hand them a sample of your product. The secret of this product is letting them try it. If they like it and experience the benefits, they will want to start using it. Here is the time to offer a sponsorship:

EXAMPLE: "John, let me have you use our XYZ Widget."

While they are trying the sample, you can tell them the benefits of your product and introduce them to network marketing.

"What type of Widgets do you use, and how large is your family? I can sell to you directly, or you can become a direct customer with the company and save 20% on your first order. By the way, I am looking for a few people that would like to earn an additional income. Could

41

you use an extra $500 to a $1,000 a month? Let me leave this little booklet with you, and I will call you tomorrow. I think you will find it interesting."

Personally, I prefer a little different approach.

EXAMPLE:

YOU: *"John, this is Ray. I want to ask a favor of you. I am involved in a new business venture, and I am quite excited about it. I would like your opinion about the product before I fully commit myself to it. Could I drop off a sample (or video) tonight? Thanks, John; I value your opinion greatly. I'll be by around 7:00. See you then!"*

When you arrive at John's home, just drop the sample or video off with the accompanying literature. Ask him to review the literature and try the product and you will call him to find out what he thinks. That's it, no more, no hype, no MLM, no Pay Plan, no information.

EXAMPLE:

YOU: *"Hi, John. Here are the samples of the Widget I am working with, and this brochure will explain it far better than I could. I have to run, but I want to thank you again for your help. I will call you tomorrow to see what you think. By the way, let your wife and children try the widget; I am anxious to see what they think. Be sure to read this little booklet. I know you will find it very interesting."*

THE FOLLOW-UP

YOU: *"Hi John, it's Ray. What did you think of the XYZ widget?"*
If you get a favorable response (meaning that he liked it), then you can take advantage of the situation like this:

YOU: *"I'm glad you feel as I do, John. I would like to get your opinion on the whole program. Would you have a little time this evening? Great! What time is best for you?"*

When you arrive, sit down and fully explain the company and compensation plan to John. If he sees what YOU saw, you will have a new distributor!

YOU: *"I knew I wasn't wrong when I saw this as a fantastic way to earn more money. The products are so good, and the compensation program is quite lucrative and without a large investment! Why don't you get in with me, and we'll work this together? You could use this to buy that motor home you've always wanted!"*

Evaluation:

What I did above was to pay John a big compliment by letting him know I valued his opinion on an important business matter. I reinforced this compliment again when I dropped off the samples and product information. When I contacted John to see what he thought of the product, I paid him another compliment by telling him how much I valued his opinion in asking him to evaluate the compensation plan. I then did the magical trick of all tricks. When I sat with John and asked that he join me in the business, I pushed his hot button by mentioning the motor home which I knew he had been wanting. I performed a smooth, nonobligatory approach by getting John to try a sample. Then I tactfully arranged for a personal meeting with him, at which time I closed the sale by suggesting he work the business to earn extra money for the motor home he had been wanting.

Teach your distributors to work their WARM List with this example, and they too will have success with the people they know.

There are many ways to build the COLD Market List. Merely by talking about your product wherever you go, you will make more contacts that you think. You are representing a product that has some degree of benefit to others, and one that you sincerely believe in. Your enthusiasm and knowledge will ultimately gain you customers, and you will sponsor a good percentage of these people into your downline. Remember that if you train your distributors to use the Three-Foot Rule, your group will grow faster than you could build it by yourself.

Please do not pre-judge your prospect list. Don't ever try to weed out the non-players. Give them all the same opportunity, and the results will surprise you. You may have a name on the list that you strongly suspect would not be a participant. However, that person may have friends or relatives that know a lot of people and could possibly lead you to those who otherwise would be inaccessible.

Do not limit possibilities to your immediate area. Most network marketing companies do not restrict you to a given area or territory. They let you build your downline sales organization anywhere in the country. If you know people in other states, call and get them started on some samples. If they need your help with a seminar, go there and help them.

Make a habit of meeting people. Be cheerful and show interest. Ask questions such as where they live, how many children they have, what they do for a living, etc. Become a "People Person." When you feel the time is right, tell them about your network business and offer a sample. If you are out and do not have samples, offer to send one in the mail. This will provide you the opportunity to obtain an address and phone number. That is half of the battle. The product will do the rest for you, provided your presentation is professional.

Trading business cards is a great way to gain new prospects and is quite easy, as everyone wants to give his/her business card away. When you ask prospects for their names and phone numbers, they may be somewhat hesitant, but by giving your business card first, they are more apt to provide you with their information.

Prospects are virtually everywhere, all around you, all of the time. They are there when you buy gasoline, shop, get a haircut, have your car serviced, buy anything from a store . . . just everywhere. It may take you a little time to discover your best cold approach to new prospects, but this is a necessity. The company you represent is great, and the products are fantastic. They will help change the lives of everyone you recruit or sell to, so what are you waiting for? Get out there and make those contacts!

What type of person am I looking for? This question is uppermost in the minds of most network marketers who are about to approach a prospect and make an attempt to secure their first distributor. Everyone has a different answer for this question: persistent, educated, organized, competitive, self-motivated, aggressive, experienced networker, etc. All of these traits are not characteristic of every successful person, but the common denominator is DESIRE. Without it, even the most qualified prospect will fail. You should not only search for people that have the DESIRE to succeed or to improve their current financial situation, but you must also help people to create the desire. Try to find people who want success as much as you do. Chances are, you will succeed faster with those who have the same desire level as you.

Change is a difficult thing for most people to accept and even more difficult to accomplish. People that are not largely successful have not altered their life styles to promote success. Those who have the desire to improve themselves often will have the best chance of success because they will be willing to make whatever changes in themselves that may be necessary to achieve success. You may have to arouse the desire in others before they can commit to a program of change. Whether it is through motivation or investigation, you must find the switch in people that will turn on that desire. Look for this switch in your first interviews with prospects and help them to discover it themselves.

Certainly, it is helpful to sponsor other networkers into your downline; many people have been highly successful by doing so. Just because someone has done network marketing in the past does not necessarily mean that he/she has the desire to make the changes necessary for a better result this time. You may still have to help some of them find their own hot button before they will make the commitment to do "Whatever it Takes" to reach their goals.

DEVELOPING PROSPECTS

Once most people have been involved in network marketing for a few months, they find themselves running out of prospects. This is the time when they must create COLD Market prospects. Creating "just prospects" is not hard to do. The right ad placed in the employment or business opportunity section of your local newspaper can generate calls and prospects. Does this type of prospecting really work? Is it profitable to advertise for prospects?

Advertising is a changing science and one that only a handful are greatly successful with. Most of the advertising we see on a daily basis is done by advertising specialists that are skilled in writing and developing an advertising campaign. There are few network marketers who can truly create those magical ads that pull thousands of prospects. Chances are that if they could produce the ad that pulled, they would not be able to close the sales. But advertising is a must in the business of networking. After all, it is the fastest way to meet new prospects. You can place an advertisement in the local newspaper this weekend and have appointments next week. If you have tried advertising, it likely didn't work as you expected. You probably wrote an ad or used one from an ad sheet furnished by your company. You possibly received a few calls and scheduled even fewer appointments. If you were lucky, you might not have had prospects hang up when they found out it was network marketing!

Proper advertising is a science that demonstrates productive techniques. First of all, you should run only "blind advertisement" (ads that do not include the name of your company or products). A good blind ad will pull far more responses than one that "tells what it is." You want your phone to ring and your voice mailbox to bulge, so run a vague or non-targeted ad designed to make the phone ring. Then, use a proper approach to "handling the call" that sets appointments with all of your qualified prospects.

There are blind advertisements in the back of this book for you to use or derive ideas from. But let's look at a few ads and see what is needed to increase the response from qualified prospects.

Look over these mini-ads and select the one you like best, or the one that you would call first. All of these ads were written to gain qualified prospects. Sure, there is copy that would produce more calls, but you would have to pre-qualify them, so why not start out with a screening of prospects in the beginning?

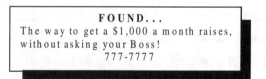

FOUND...
The way to get a $1,000 a month raises,
without asking your Boss!
777-7777

If we look at this ad, we see the word FOUND in bold caps. People will have a natural curiosity and read the ad. Now it talks about a $1,000 a month raise, and there is a phone number. This ad will bring calls from curious people. You will have to qualify most of them, but it will also pull a better quality caller because it is a thinker's ad and a curious person's ad. Curious people will certainly want to know more about earning a $1,000 a month raise. Is this ad a great one to run this weekend? It could be. You will certainly have some prospects to practice on and, who knows, you may sponsor one or two!

In these two ads, you are reaching into the hearts and souls of many people who wish they could. You will also receive calls from people that have a sense of humor. You are starting to reach the audience you need to reach: people with personalities!

Wouldn't everyone like to work at home? At least, it is on everyone's mind right now. You also mention the word entrepreneur and that they are wanted. Maybe you should say, "Entrepreneurs NOT wanted." But the importance of this ad copy is in the body. "We provide the Opportunity, Training and Motivation. You provide yourself." This looks interesting because of the words TRAINING, MOTIVATION, AND OPPORTUNITY. This will pull better qualified callers.

We led with
humor so will
attract callers
with a person-
ality and also
those looking
for a GREAT

second income or full-time potential. The body of the ad also tells
them that you Train, Coach, and Help. The ad also refers to an appointment. This ad will attract better-qualified prospects. The "for
appointment" will create a professional atmosphere and place the
call in your hands from the beginning.

Simple; you
are advertis-
ing a second
income op-
portunity.

This ad is designed to attract working people.

Now here is a great ad! It has everything you need. The announce-
ment line states your deal, EXTRA INCOME. Then, we have fun in the
body: "Divorced, Bad Credit or No Spouse and Good Credit, WE
DON'T CARE!" Next, it tells about the training and hands-on help.

Also, it states "For Appointment Call" and lists the phone number.

All of these are good inexpensive ads that you can keep running week after week. When you are new and starting out with ads, you need the practice. So choose one and try it.

The calls will arrive soon after the advertising breaks. This is when you need to be prepared and ready. Far too many times the networker is slow to return a call from a voice machine or a voice mailbox, and the prospect has cooled off. You must contact all ad responders as soon as possible. They mustered the courage and interest to make the call, so you should respond quickly.

Set up your workplace to create a positive, high-energy atmosphere. There should be no background noises and interruptions during the call. Planning ahead will be the key to a smooth response call. If you have children, make sure their needs are taken care of before you make the call.

If you are answering the calls directly and are not routing them through a voice mail or telephone answering system, you should answer in a professional manner. "Good morning" or "Good afternoon" are always good ways to answer. You should never answer with a company name or use your company's name when answering the phone. You never want to "give away" or "leak" the company or opportunity before the interview.

You must understand a few fundamental reasons why people respond to your advertising plus a little about their personalities. By dividing ad callers into three classifications, we find that we can prescreen prospects during their initial calls.

1. Job seekers: There will always be those prospects that are simply calling every number in the paper looking for a job. These are usually deadbeat prospects that won't even show up for an interview. You will learn from experience how to screen these from other callers. Usually, they give themselves away early in the conversation by asking how much the job pays and what hours they would have to work.

2. Serious prospects: These people have taken the initiative to do something about increasing their financial situation and are usually upbeat and will show up for an interview. Do not waste your time with those who do not show initiative on the phone or sound like they are not really interested. If they have energy in their voices, they have potential.

3. Reverse sponsoring networkers: You will certainly have these types calling your advertising. They are people working other MLM programs who do not advertise, but call those who do and try to sponsor them into their programs. You simply do not have time to deal with these types, and it certainly indicates that these people do not have good ethics. They would not appreciate your wasting their time, but they don't mind wasting yours. You will learn to recognize these immediately, so just brush them off. Tell them if they want to spend money like you did and run an advertisement, you will call if you are interested.

Out of all the possibly excellent prospects for your opportunity who read your advertising, only a small percent will actually call. This is human nature and is just a fact of life. However, those who did show the initiative to call will certainly make better co-workers than those who did not.

The following is an average call from advertising:

YOU: *"Good Morning, this is Ray. How may I help you?"*

PROSPECT: *"Hello, I am calling about the advertisement in the paper concerning earning a second income. Can you tell me about it?"*

YOU: *"I would love to; but first, let me get your name and phone number. I am in the middle of an interview and will call you back in a few minutes."*

This is a great way to do two important things. You will obtain their names and phone numbers and when you call them back, you will be directly in charge of the conversation.

YOU: *"Hello, this is Ray, and I would like to speak with John."*

PROSPECT: *"This is John."*

YOU: *"I am returning a call you made to me today concerning a second income advertisement in the paper. I will need to schedule you for a short interview and overview. What is your schedule?"*

PROSPECT: *"Can you tell me a little about it over the phone?"*

YOU: *"We do not do telephone interviews, but I can tell you this: I represent a major company that is expanding in this area. It is an excellent chance for you to get started building a second or full-time income. Let me ask you a few questions. What occupation are you currently involved in? How much time could you devote to a second income opportunity? Would you be willing to train? There are also some start-up fees that you will be required to pay. If this turns out to be something that you wish to pursue, I will make sure you recover that in the first few weeks. I do need to know before our interview just how much money you would like to earn on a monthly basis."*

PROSPECT: *"Is this Multilevel?"*

YOU: *"Were you looking for a multilevel opportunity?"* (Answer this question with a question. Stay In Control.)

PROSPECT: *"No, I have tried that in the past, and I just lost money."*

YOU: *"Let me schedule you for an appointment; then, I can show you what we are doing and the level of support we offer. I think you will get excited after our meeting."* DO NOT RESPOND TO THE SUBJECT OF MLM if it can be avoided.

Now, schedule the appointment and be ready when he/she arrives for the interview. You should have made the following notes on this conversation: name; telephone number; present occupation; asked if it were MLM; how much he/she wants to earn a month; did an MLM and failed. Describe the level of enthusiasm the prospect had over the phone, etc.

You will use this information during the interview.

The key to successful telephone technique when answering advertising responses is to Stay In Charge of the Conversation. Answer all questions with a question. NEVER try to explain anything about your program over the phone. SET the interview. If you lose control of the conversation, you will lose the prospect. Remember that you are the professional; the caller is the prospect.

In the above example of answering ad responses, you are screening or qualifying your prospect and, at the same time, are gathering pertinent information about him/her. For example, you have explained that there will be training, time commitments, and initial start-up expenses. These three statements will pre-qualify anyone that schedules an interview. The prospects who actually show up for the interview will know that they will need to be trained, devote a certain amount of time to the business, and spend some initial money to get started.

Let me share an important story that changed the way I did MLM and the methods of sponsoring. I joined an MLM Opportunity in September of 1990. It was not my first and proved not to be my last. I learned the product line and compensation plan, developed my presentation to prospects, and started out building my downline. I reached the "Executive" level with the company after only 3 days. By the end of the first month, using this system, I had developed a downline sales organization consisting of eighty-four distributors. At the end of my fifth month, my income was crowding three thousand dollars. I was feeling good about myself and what I was developing. Then, I met Bill.

Bill was an Executive distributor like myself who had been involved with the company only a month longer than I had. The big difference was that he was earning a little over ten thousand dollars a month. What was he doing that I wasn't? I had developed this system that was duplicating all through my downline, and my commission checks were growing each month. What was I missing?

When I ask Bill what he was doing that had built his check so fast with about the same number of distributors, he invited me to come over the next morning and find out. Bill also told me that he had an appointment set with a prospect at 10:30 A.M. and that I should arrive at 10. By noon the next day, I knew Bill's system, and it was good -- so good that I immediately started using it myself. Bill advertised, and had developed a different approach. He explained that he never told an ad caller that it was a MLM business; rather, he maintained control during the phone conversation and set an appointment.

Bill's 10:30 prospect arrived with his wife, right on time. Bill introduced himself and me and invited them into his office. He asked what they were looking for in a second income opportunity and noted it on a note pad. He also asked each of them what they did for a living and what they did in their spare time, and made notes. Next, he explained network marketing like this:

"There are several ways to obtain a second income. One way is to work a second job, or work longer hours at your present jobs (talking to both husband and wife). Another is to change jobs for a better paying one, but chances are you would not be able to find one that would pay you the thousand dollars you want to make. The third way is to find a way to leverage your efforts with other people and share in these collective efforts. J. Paul Getty once said something to the effect that he would rather have one percent of the efforts of one hundred people

than one hundred percent of his own. There are only two ways to accomplish this, and they are either to buy a franchise that you could employ one hundred people in, or to develop a network marketing sales organization with one hundred people.

"Franchises are great and work for a lot of people, but what about all of us who do not have hundreds of thousands of dollars to invest in a franchise? Well, there is an entire industry of network marketing companies that offer people like us the opportunity to invest a minimal amount of money and, with sweat equity, build a lucrative full or part-time second income. Think of it as referral marketing. You bought an appliance last week from Fred's Fast Refrigerators. You liked it so well and the price was lower than you found anywhere else, so you told everyone you knew about it. Out of the people you told, seven went to Fred's Fast Refrigerators and bought new refrigerators. Did you receive a commission check from referring seven sales to Fast Fred? I didn't think so! Well, when you refer someone to a network marketing product or service, you will receive a referral bonus. We have all done network marketing all of our lives; we just did not get paid for it.

"You see, network marketing companies do not advertise and do not distribute their products through jobbers. This money normally paid to jobbers and wholesalers is paid to independent distributors just like you and me. So for a small registration fee, you can become an independent distributor with one of these companies and earn referral commissions merely by referring others to its program. Now you and I both know that most people who become involved with these companies don't do as well as they would like. Here is where our system comes into place (go to the flip chart and show the goal sheets).

"You see, this system gives you a step-by-step map of building a super structure that will create your team and develop the income you desire. The key to this system is that I will be your sponsor and will be making presentations with you. In this manner, we will sponsor your first two distributors; then, we will help them to sponsor their first two; and next, we will sponsor your third.

"My commitment to you is to help you complete each goal sheet until you have reached the Executive level in our company. By this time, you will have been trained in this system and in making presentations to prospects. Now, even after you become an Executive, I will be there for you any time you need my help. There are also other upline leaders that you will meet who will help you just by calling them. So you see, although you are in business for yourself, you will never be by yourself."

Bill would then turn to his prospect(s) and say: *"What I would like for you to do is take this training book home with you and read it. This will explain how our system works and just what you will have to do over the next few weeks to earn your first commission check. You do want to start out earning commission checks each month, don't you? Now this training material is only $20, which is one of the best investments you will ever make.*

"The company I represent is ..." Bill explains all about his company and the opportunity. He also gives his prospect(s) several entry levels to choose from.

With this presentation system, Bill was able to start his distributors out with a full complement of products, whereas I had been sponsoring my prospects with the bare minimum. The difference was only in sales volume between our commission checks. I immediately added Bill's interview technique to my presentations and soon saw the difference in my monthly earnings. I also noticed that Bill's organization sold many more products than mine. They had the inventory of products to show and sell; mine did not.

I do not recommend your inviting total strangers to your home for presentations like Bill did. Rather, select a nice restaurant close to your home and use it for your interviews. Check with the manager and tell him/her you like to conduct short interviews with clients over coffee. Ask what the slack times are, and try to schedule your interviews during this period. Meet with the staff and explain what you do (interviews). Tell them that you tip well, but would like not to be bothered during your interviews. This will help you to create a more professional presentation. Most employees and management will greet you as a regular, which helps your image with your prospect. You may even pick up a few distributors from the staff as well!

This is the world of professional network marketing. Treat it like a profession, and it will treat you favorably.

Advertising can be expensive, and the smaller ads do not pull as well as the larger ones do. You can create an advertising co-op from within your downline distributors, pool an equal amount of advertising dollars each week or month, and place a small display ad in your local paper.

This is an example of a medium energy display ad designed to produce prospects that know there is a minimum of $80 start-up expense. Your co-op group can work together to deal with the prospects that call from this advertisement.

Prospect qualifying through advertising is one method of gaining qualified prospects. Say, for instance, you ran one of the following ads in the help wanted section of the newspaper:

Let's say that your advertising cost $75 for the weekend edition. You would need only fifteen calls to break even in the cost of the ads, BUT you would have fifteen prospects reviewing the material. With a great cover letter, you might receive a response from all fifteen, and every one could possibly be QUALIFIED! Now, depending on the area you are advertising in, you could conceivably pull twice or even three times as many responses. This could make advertising profitable, and with a large number purchasing the qualifying material, you would have a good list of qualified prospects to introduce to your XYZ business opportunity.

In the above examples, you are actually qualifying everyone who reads the advertisement. The prospects that purchase the book have taken the first step toward qualifying. The next step is making the call. Now, if you consider that everyone who purchases a book may be qualified, then you should instigate a follow-up call.

YOU: *"Hello, My name is Ray. You purchased the booklet from me entitled* 'How To Get Rich Without Winning The Lottery,' *by Keith Schreiter, and I am following up with you to see if you might be interested in earning additional income."*

If your conversation goes well, you should set an appointment. Proper telephone techniques can be found in Tom Paredes's audio cassette album entitled "Telephone Techniques," which is available at www.mlmroadmap.com or from KAAS Publishing. There are many secrets and "tricks of the trade" when it comes to proper telephone techniques. By purchasing Tom's tapes, you can learn from one of the industry's masters.

Since your advertisement brought in profits, you should also consider sending one of the "Are You Walking Past A Fortune?" booklets, by Tom "Big Al" Schreiter, with each "How To Get Rich" book. Both of these publications are great tools for explaining the principles of network marketing in a very subtle manner. Remember also that many people will value written material over conversation. These may be purchased from www.mlmroadmap.com or KAAS Publishing, P.O. Box 890084, Houston, Texas 77289 (281) 280-9800.

CHAPTER 5
THE $100,000 CLOSE

No matter how many WARM Market prospects you generate, or how well you do in COLD Market prospecting, the sale always needs a close. It has been said that closing is an art, and that may be true. Most of the highest earners in any sales positions are always the best closers. Therefore, you must be able to close your prospects and sponsor them into your business. Closing is something you can learn to do; and once you make your first close, more will follow.

You will be spending much of your time finding prospects in the beginning, but as soon as you have developed even a small downline sales organization, your job will be to help your distributors close prospects into their sales organizations. To learn to close, you must first understand exactly what you must overcome with prospects in order to make the sale.

Look back on yourself and write down the objections that came to mind when you listened to your first presentation about XYZ Widget Company. What was said or explained that made you say "YES"? What did your sponsor say that melted away your resistance? Ask this of other distributors you meet. Look for these objections and overcoming answers, and you will develop answers for everyone. Even though your prospects will have various levels of resistance and different reasons for saying "NO," there is one approach that seems to work with most prospects. I call this the "$100,000 Close." Most independent distributors with network marketing companies share the belief that it is possible to earn $100,000 a year in this business. Many do, and many try. Nevertheless, the potential is certainly there with most network marketing companies, and this amount seems to be a commonplace goal with many distributors.

Most prospects have five questions that must be answered before they are ready for a close. These are:

1. Who is the company?
2. What are the products?
3. How much money can I earn?
4. How much will it cost me?
5. Can I do this?

Prior to the $100,000 close, you must answer these five questions for your prospects without their asking. Therefore you should incorporate the answers into your presentation.

YOU: *"Let me first explain exactly what I do. You might call me a representative for a research and development company. I share the* company's products with my friends, family, and people I come in contact with like you. The more people I help to earn money, the more I earn.

"The company I work with is XYZ Widget Company, located in MLM, Arizona. It is a research and development company that has developed a quality line of Widgets. The company is a debt free, privately owned corporation with sales of one million dollars a week. Its products are marketed through a network of independent distributors like you and me. There are no territories, bosses, or pressures.

"XYZ Widget Company started out at the President's kitchen table eight years ago and has really grown fast. This was due primarily to the quality of its Widgets and the immediate acceptance they had in the marketplace.

"Our flagship Widget is our Super Widget (place the product in the prospect's hand). Most people can see the difference that the Super Widget makes in less than two weeks, and we have a customer for life! The prices on all of the Widgets are very reasonable compared to those of our competitors. Quality is the secret with XYZ Widgets.

"Although there is really no limit to an individual's earning potential with XYZ Widget Company, most part-time distributors can easily earn between $500 and $1,500 per month. This is a good second income for most families, but the potential is definitely there to earn much more. It all depends on what you want and how much you want it. This is the way our distributor compensation works (very briefly go over the highlights), so you can see that we are paid directly on product movement within our downline sales organizations. The exciting thing *is that your income will come from the collective efforts of everyone in your sales organization, not just your own. This means should you get sick for a long period, you are still earning from the collective efforts of your downline sales organization. Once you develop an organization, it is yours for life and, should anything happen to you, your spouse and children will inherit it and continue to receive commission and bonus checks. You see, when you become an XYZ Widget Independent Distributor, you are in business for yourself, but not by yourself. The secret we have all learned is that we create success by helping others. I will be helping you start your downline sales organization by going with you and helping you make presentations.. After we have done this ten or so times, you will not only have a group of your own distributors to work with, but also you will have learned how to work with them from watching me. I will always be there for you if you need any help along the way. We also have others in our upline that are most willing to help.*

"Now most people ask me how much it will cost for them to get started, should they see an opportunity here. The Distributor kit is $65 and contains everything you need to know about the company, products, and marketing plan. You will also need an initial supply of Widgets. You cannot effectively sell to others from an empty wagon , and you need to become a product of the product yourself. We do have a recommended start-up package for new distributors that consists of the distributor kit and twelve Widgets. This is a $825 value that you get for only $325. You will most likely sell this initial supply in our first week of presentations, because I will be helping you. Almost all of my new distributors show a profit during the first week of presentations because the Widgets are so good that many of the prospects buy one during the presentation.

"Now, if you are anything at all like me, you are probably thinking to yourself - 'Can I do this; I mean can I really do this?' Let me stress that I am going to be there with you as long as it takes for you to build your foundation. We have a step-by-step system that assures success." Show this book and system and what a downline sales organization will look like after the fourth step.

THE $100,000 Close:

YOU: *"Let me ask you something. If you make the decision right now to become an XYZ Widget distributor, how much would you want to earn, let's say, on a monthly basis?"*

Write the amount your prospect wants to earn down on a note pad. For example, that he/she tells you $5,000 a month.

YOU: *"OK, you want to earn $5,000 a month becoming an XYZ distributor, and you will be building a downline sales organization sharing the XYZ Widgets with friends and family to earn it. Realistically, when do you want this?"*

You have just asked the second question of the $100,000 Close, "When?" Suppose your prospect tells you in three months.

YOU: *"OK, three months it is; I am making a note of that. How much are you making right now from your present job? What do you think your boss would say if you ask for a $5,000 raise? I thought so! Now if you got started with me today, and you were making an additional $1,500 a month three months from now, would you quit or keep on working to earn more?"*

Most prospects will say they would keep on working. This can also be used to tone down a prospect's monetary goal for a period. Suppose your green prospect wanted to earn $50,000 a month by the third month. Perhaps it is good for all of your prospects to want $50,000 a month income, but how realistic is it? If anyone joins your sales group with the expectation of earning $50,000 a month in three months, he/she will likely be disappointed and quit when it does not happen. Using this approach will enable you to bring the prospect closer to reality and get a commitment.

YOU: *"The reason I ask that most people give me a one year commitment to this business is because by following our system, they surprise themselves a lot earlier. How about you? If I give you my commitment to help you build your foundation over the next few weeks and teach you what you need to know, would you give me a one year commitment to do this business in order to earn $5,000 a month?"*

Most prospects will say "YES" at this point. Now, you must ask the third question in the $100,000 Close.

YOU*: "What are you willing to do in order to earn $5,000 a month with XYZ Widget Company?"*

No matter what they answer, write it down and then tell them:

YOU: *"What I am going to ask of you is simple. Would you be willing to go back to school one night a week for an hour? Would you be willing to work with me in your spare time over the next few weeks to build a foundation for your organization? Would you be willing to commit to doing this business for one year? Would you be willing to invest $80 in* *a distributor manual and $325 in initial product? Would you be willing to purchase a minimum of $XXX per month in order to earn $5,000 a month?"*

You should receive a "YES" to these questions, so you are ready for the $100,000 Close!

YOU: *"Great! When do you want to get started earning your first $5,000?"*

You will be surprised at the number of prospects that will answer "NOW"! The next step is to place the application in front of them and then complete an order form. Closing is guaranteed at this time, for they have made the commitment.

YOU: *"I think you have filled out everything that we need. How do you wish to pay for your first order?"*

By properly preparing your prospect for the close, you will increase your closing success. This prospect was first prepared by answering the five questions in the initial presentation.

1. Who is the company?   4. How much does it cost?
2. What are the products?   5. Can I do it?
3. How much money can I earn?

Then you immediately work the $100,000 Close.

Looking back on the initial presentation, you will notice that the prospect was reassured that he/she would not be alone in the beginning because you were committed to help with presentations for the first few weeks. You also stated that there were a number of upline distributors also willing to help. This is worth 50% of any close. Every prospect will feel more comfortable joining with a mentor and a coach for guidance.

The prospect was also shown and explained the step-by-step system, which reassured that there would be a definite and clear blueprint to follow from the very beginning.

1. What or how much do you want to earn?
2. When do you want this?
3. What are you willing to do to get it?
4. When do you want to get started earning?

The interaction you created with the four questions in the $100,000 Close served to create a mental bond and get the prospect into a responsive role, rather than just listening to your presentation. Every answer will be positive in nature and lead to saying "RIGHT NOW" to the last question. If you do not interact with prospects and get them thinking and talking, you will not succeed in making a close.

This presentation is highly effective with 90% of prospects, but there are still those that are unmovable. Usually these are the ones who do not have enough available cash to get started and may be embarrassed about the fact. I sometimes believe that the harder it is for someone to join, the better he/she will do. So, work with that prospect and make it easier to join. Such prospects are sometimes the ones that can produce those great referrals. Never miss the opportunity to get referrals.

YOU: *"If you need to wait a few weeks to put your money together, I can understand. I will just hold your application out until you can afford to make your purchase. Meanwhile, we can go ahead and start making presentations so you will have an organization started when you are ready. This will assure that you will be able to pay for your initial products when you receive them and make your first profit with XYZ Widget Company at the same time. You should get this book right now and study it. This is the system we will be working with to build your income."*

Show the Prospect Generator and how to create a list of prospects. Suggest purchasing this book to pick up some basic training before getting started.

No matter what reasons prospects give for not "writing the check" today, seize the opportunity to make referral presentations. Chances are that if you have them accompany you on a few presentations to their prospects, you will get that check quickly. At the very least, you will have the opportunity to make a few referral presentations to people you would not ever have met.

A "Force Close" technique that seems to work quite well is to create fear of loss.

YOU: *"Now earning $5,000 a month with XYZ Widget Company is not for everyone and may not be right for you. The only reason I showed this to you today is that I am committed to making it work for everyone that works with me. If it is not something you want to do, that's fine, but I am sure you know someone that you could introduce me to who would be interested."*

The "Take Away Close" is sometimes very effective.

YOU: *"My income depends entirely on the success I have with all of my distributors. That's why I spend so much time getting them started before I let them work by themselves. I can only work with one or two new distributors at a time, so if this is something that you do not want, I will completely understand and appreciate your telling me right up front and not wasting my time. I will just find someone else that wants it. By the way, if you are not interested, who do you know that might like for me to help them earn $5,000 a month?"*

Should you strike out completely, don't let it bother you at all. There are some people that will never get to where they want to be in life because they have a fear of some kind that prevents them from trying.

"Some Will, Some Won't, So What . . . NEXT"

CHAPTER 6

STRUCTURE BUILDING

You should now have an understanding of how to get started with your network marketing business. You will begin to sponsor new distributors, especially if you have an upline sponsor that really knows the business. "WHERE DO YOU PLACE THEM?" and "HOW DO YOU BUILD FOR PROFIT?" are possibly the two most asked questions when sponsoring the first distributors to your organization. At least, they were mine. It cost me a lot of lost commissions and heartaches to learn the answers, and here they are:

You must build a solid foundation of distributors in your sales organization or downline -- ones who are not only loyal to YOU, but also to the PRODUCT and COMPANY you are working. This means that they will follow your leadership and the company directives, even if the company makes a few changes or modifications. Remember that nothing is forever, and this is very true for network marketing businesses. To think any other way is foolish. How do you build this kind of organization? Simple - - follow the building system and teach everyone in your organization to do the same. The process is called DUPLICATION! This word is a fundamental KEY to network marketing. The building system is easily duplicated and can be taught quickly to all members of your organization.

You purchased this book with the building system, so duplicate it with everyone in your organization and all new distributors, and teach them to do the same. They all need a copy. New distributors are often easier to work with than seasoned ones. They are eager to learn and are ready to build a business to add those extra dollars to their monthly income. Seasoned distributors are often hesitant to purchase training aids, especially when they have not been successful with their other network marketing endeavors. Many are not as successful as they expected to be, or more important, not as successful as they were told they would be by the speaker at their first network marketing opportunity meeting. Too many quality people give up before they get started, and that is a terrible shame. At any rate, duplicate the purchase of this book and building system so that everyone possible in your organization will have a copy. Now, here we go!

The building system is composed of 4 primary STEPS. These are the STEPS TO SUCCESS in network marketing. There are no time limits; you may work each step at your own pace. Those of you who want to grow fast will move faster than those who do not. The building system sets an easy pace of achievement for you. Your FIRST STEP will be to sponsor two distributors. In theory, as a new distributor, you will have more personally known prospects to choose from during the first few weeks or months than at any other time in your network marketing career. Therefore, you can easily complete the first step of sponsoring two distributors. If you are new to this business, ask your sponsor for help in sponsoring your first two distributors. You supply the prospects or leads and let your sponsor show you the ropes.

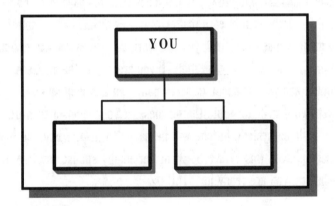

STEP ONE

Your FIRST STEP in the building system is to sponsor two distributors into your program. Prepare yourself with product knowledge, company knowledge, and an organized plan of action when making a presentation. Using your WARM List of prospects, or any list of prospects you may have in front of you, choose 5 people to contact about your business opportunity. If you are working from your WARM List and know these people, you should try to choose the ones who are energetic and have a desire to achieve more out of life. Schedule a time and place (preferably in their homes) to meet and discuss the product and the business opportunity. You must determine before this meeting which direction you will take, whether it is starting with the opportunity or the product. You will be teaching the duplication of this process hundreds of times as you build your organization, so learn the system well.

Your goal is to sponsor 2 people into your downline sales organization and teach them this duplication process. The goal may be set for your first month, week, or day. This depends on how fast you want your organization to grow and how much time you have to spend with it. If you truly want to earn that extra money or build an organization to make you self-sufficient, you will work as hard as you can to build your downline sales organization. If you are new to the business, you should ask your sponsor to accompany you and help sponsor your first two distributors into the business. If your sponsor is working the building system, he/she will be happy to help. When you have accomplished this FIRST STEP of personally sponsoring two distributors, you are ready for STEP #2.

"Don't approach without a coach"

"On the phone never alone"

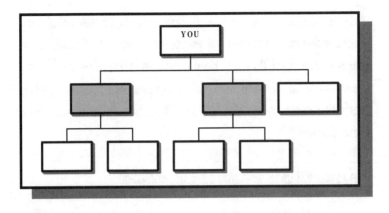

White = New Distributors   Screened = Old Distributors

STEP TWO

Your SECOND STEP is to help each of your two distributors sponsor two new distributors. You must give encouragement and support, so they can get started immediately. A quick success here can set the stage for many more to come. If you make the mistake some distributors do and let your new distributors cool off, you may never be able to get them started. Remember that they will be strongest if you work with them immediately! They need to see you at work so they can duplicate. This is the best form of training.

You must duplicate this process with every distributor you sponsor and train them to do the same. After you have helped each of your two new distributors sponsor two distributors, you will need to follow through with the same program as before. Call the next morning after sponsoring and reinforce the decision they made to join your program. Meet to discuss their plan of action, and arrange to accompany and help both of them to sponsor their first two distributors. You should contact all new distributors in your downline soon after they are sponsored and welcome them aboard. Realizing that their sponsor is not as experienced as you are, you should provide the necessary support they will need during their first few weeks as a new distributor. You will work with them and their sponsors to help each one sponsor two distributors. Now, you sponsor your third new distributor.

In essence, this is what you have accomplished:

1. You sponsored two new distributors.
2. You helped these new distributors each sponsor two new distributors.
3. You sponsored your third new distributor.

You will now repeat this process with your third new distributor and help him/her to sponsor 2 new distributors.

"Don't approach without a coach"

"On the phone never alone"

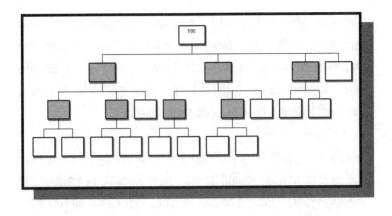

White = New Distributors   Screened = Old Distributors

STEP THREE

Work with your third new distributor to sponsor two new distributors, and help your first two distributors work with their two new distributors to sponsor two each. Help the first two distributors to sponsor their third. YOU sponsor your fourth.

By now, you must have realized that each step in the building system is duplicated by each of your distributors. They are always following the same system, and YOU are setting the example. The steps of your distributors will be determined by their starting dates. They are always to sponsor two new distributors first and work with these two until they have duplicated before sponsoring a third. This pattern of the building system will allow every distributor to grow in width and in depth at the same time. They will build a strong foundation by helping their first level distributors to do the same. Network marketing distributors with strong foundations in their organizations will reach success and stay there.

This step gets a little more complex, as your organization is now growing. From this point forward, you will start a supervisory role with some of your first distributors. They will have been in the program for some time and should have learned quite a lot from you. They will have this book to guide them along.

Telephone support every few days and a conference before or after the weekly meeting should be enough to keep them working the building system. You will be concentrating your efforts on your newest distributor and helping him/her sponsor two new distributors.

Notice how your downline is growing in width and depth at the same time, and your first distributors are only one month behind you. They are duplicating your previous month.

"Don't approach without a coach"

"On the phone never alone"

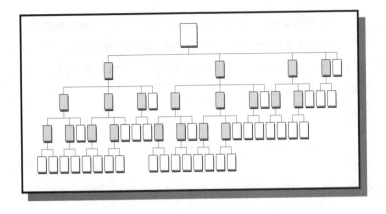

White = New Distributors   Shaded = Old Distributors

STEP FOUR

1. Support your first two distributors by telephone while they take over as leaders of their own organizations. As such, they will work the building system by duplicating your efforts.

2. Work with your third distributor to help his/her two distributors each sponsor two new distributors and then sponsor a third.

3. Help your fourth distributor sponsor two new distributors.

4. You sponsor your fifth distributor.

Taking a look at what you have accomplished in the first 4 steps by using this building system, we see that you personally sponsored 5 people into your business. You worked with these 5, using their contacts and leads to build a downline sales organization of 54 distributors. What happened to those MLM war stories that say you must sponsor hundreds of people in order to earn commissions? The secret is that you are working with your downline, helping them grow. You, of course, benefit from the growth of your distributors and your downline.

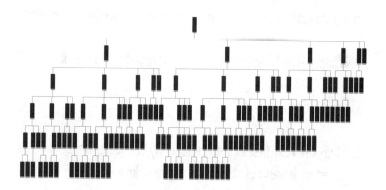

After completing the four primary steps, you can continue with additional steps in the same manner. The above is what your downline sales organization will look like if you completed a FIFTH STEP. Please notice how you are growing in depth and width. This is proportional growth and builds leaders each month. Your leaders will develop both in depth and in width.

Good Luck on your Journey and . . .
"Remember, Success is a JOURNEY, NOT a Destination."

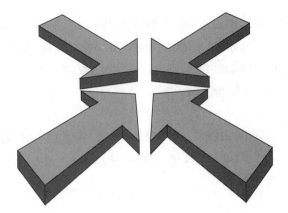

CHAPTER 7

PRINCIPLES OF THE SYSTEM

STRUCTURE

This system is a structure or blueprint of where and when to place new distributors in your downline sales organization. A review and further study of the Goal Sheets will illustrate their strategic role in making the system work so well. It will be necessary for you to help all of your new distributors sponsor their new distributors when they first get started. You are not only helping with the growth of your organization, but also you are conducting a mini-training meeting each time you make a presentation with a member of your downline. This mini-training is very powerful, as it serves to organize your distributors and teach them to work together. There are two phrases that you should note to memory and repeat often with all of your distributors: "Don't approach without a coach" and "On the phone, never alone." This system teaches the two on one, or the third party presentation, with the upline sponsor making the presentation. This principle has built more downlines than any other technique in the network marketing industry.

Compensation plans differ, and therefore, your goal sheets will be structured according to the plan your company uses. These plans are described below:

UNILEVEL (Unlimited Width Plan)

The unilevel is one of the earliest forms of network marketing compensation structures. These plans allow distributors to sponsor an unlimited number of first generation (or level) distributors. Compensation is earned from the first five to eight levels with five being the most common. Fixed and sometimes varying percentages are paid on sales volume on each pay level. It is the total of these percentages that ultimately determines the maximum payout to the field of distributors. Some unilevel plans have roll-ups, compression, and/or infinity bonuses. This allows top distributors to qualify for deeper level commissions until downline leaders achieve higher recognition and also qualify for deeper commissions. Some current pay plans also incorporate an "infinity bonus." This can be misleading, as infinity is only to the next distributor with equal qualification. Volume accumulates through the end of the month, and generally checks are issued once per month. There are also companies offering "Matching Bonuses" based on the performance of personally sponsored distributors.

STAIR-STEP BREAK-A-WAY (Unlimited Width Plan)

The stair-step break-a-way plan is an unlimited width plan, allowing distributors to sponsor an unlimited number of people on their front line (first generation). Many stair-step break-a-way plans have width requirements to reach volume in depth and large quotas and group volume requirements. These plans are loaded with individual qualifiers that distributors must earn in order to derive higher commissions in the plan. Usually they pay five to seven levels deep, and commissions are earned from fixed percentage amounts paid on sales volume. It is the total of these percentages, according to the limited levels, that determines the maximum payout of this form of plan. The break-a-way plan derived its name because of the fact that when a distributor reaches a certain volume level, his/her entire group breaks away from their commission group. Some plans allow you to continue to earn a small percentage of the sales volume that this break-a-way group attains. Some distributors coined the phrase "Break-a-way is Take-a-way" because their commissions either stopped or diminished after the break-a-way occurred.

MATRIX PLANS

In general, Matrix plans limit the number of first generation (level) placements. In a Matrix, you could be limited to, for example, three people on your first level and twelve levels deep. This would be called a 3x12 Matrix. Because there are many variations of width and depth combinations in the Matrix plans, there are no defined Goal Sheets for the Matrix. You can use the unlimited width Goal Sheets to plot the Matrix plans.

BINARY PLANS

The binary compensation structure is basically an unlimited depth, two-wide matrix. You can place only two people on your first level. Everyone else goes beneath those people. Binary commissions are earned by accumulating a specified maximum amount of sales volume. This sales volume may accumulate over an unlimited period of time. There is no depth limit in the binary plan. Every sale will accumulate toward the specified amount of sales volume requirement. The number of levels between you and a given recruit is not important. The factor determining whether you get a commission from that person is not what level he/she is on, but rather how much commissionable sales volume is generated in the levels between you and that person.

Each tracking position is divided into a left and a right, and the binary plans issue commission earnings based on a pre-defined match of sales volume. There are no group volume requirements or quotas. Binary plans require legs to be balanced. Average payout is 10% on unlimited depth. Some plans pay out as much as 20% on unlimited levels if all legs are balanced. Because of product costs, there are variations from plan to plan. Some binary plans pay on equal volume matches (50/50), meaning that volume needs to balance on each side to receive a commission check that week. Other plans have a 1/3 - 2/3 split, meaning you can have up to 66% of your volume on the strong side and still match with 33% on the weak leg. All plans have a daily or weekly limit. This daily or weekly limit is pre-defined in the tracking software and is the ultimate key which sets the maximum distributor payout.

Unilevel, stair-step break-a-ways, and matrix plans pay commissions on all purchases that occur through a specified maximum number of levels (generally five to twelve), regardless of how small or large a cash amount that might be. Binary plans turn that around. They pay off on all sales that occur through a specified maximum dollar amount regardless of how many levels away they accumulate from.

We will first show how to structure your downline for the Unilevel and Stair-Step Break-A-Way Plans (Unlimited Width). Later, in Chapter 8, you will learn how to place your distributors in the Binary Plan.

GOAL SHEETS

The following pages are goal sheets to use in following the four primary steps of the system. Use these as flip charts showing prospects and new distributors the building system. Show them how by helping their upline and downline distributors with this step-by-step building system, they will build a downline sales organization that has a strong foundation - - one developed proportionally in width and depth. A downline sales organization built by design will continue to grow and become a Road Map for all who use it.When you have a position completed, color that position with the following color codes:

1st Goal Sheet, Color BLUE.   3rd Goal Sheet, Color RED.
2nd Goal Sheet, Color YELLOW.   4th Goal Sheet, Color PURPLE.

This will allow you to see at a glance when a certain position is filled, according to the color of that position.

"Remember - - -
A flawless blueprint has value ONLY when it is implemented with knowledge and perseverance."

1st GOAL SHEET
Unlimited Width Plan

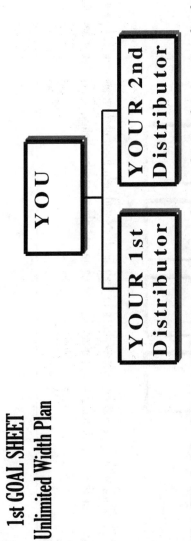

```
                    YOU
           ┌─────────┴─────────┐
    YOUR 1st            YOUR 2nd
   Distributor          Distributor
```

STEP 1. With the help of your sponsor, make presentations to those you know and sponsor two distributors. Place their names and phone numbers below. Color these new distributors BLUE.

NAME _____

PHONE _____

NAME _____

PHONE _____

2nd GOAL SHEET
Unlimited Width Plan

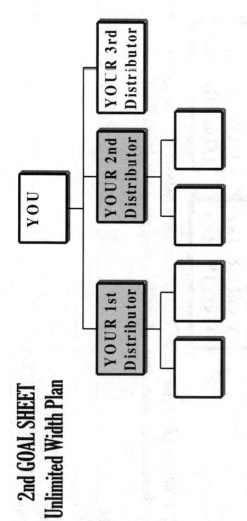

STEP 2. Work with them, making presentations to their contacts and help them each to sponsor two new distributors. You sponsor your third new distributor and place his/her name and phone number below. Color these new distributors YELLOW.

NAME _____

PHONE _____

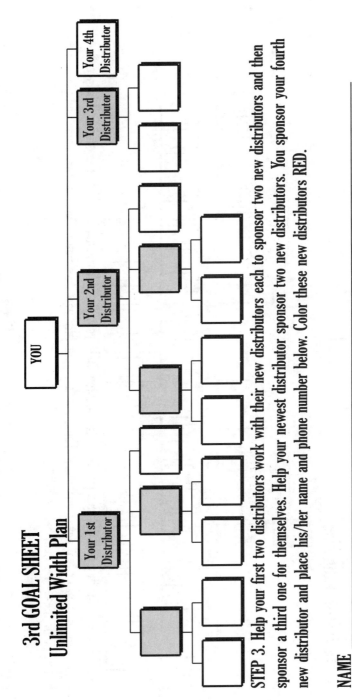

3rd GOAL SHEET
Unlimited Width Plan

YOU

Your 1st Distributor

Your 2nd Distributor

Your 3rd Distributor

Your 4th Distributor

STEP 3. Help your first two distributors work with their new distributors and then sponsor a third one for themselves. Help your newest distributor sponsor two new distributors. You sponsor your fourth new distributor and place his/her name and phone number below. Color these new distributors RED.

NAME _____

PHONE _____

91

4th GOAL SHEET
Unlimited Width Plan

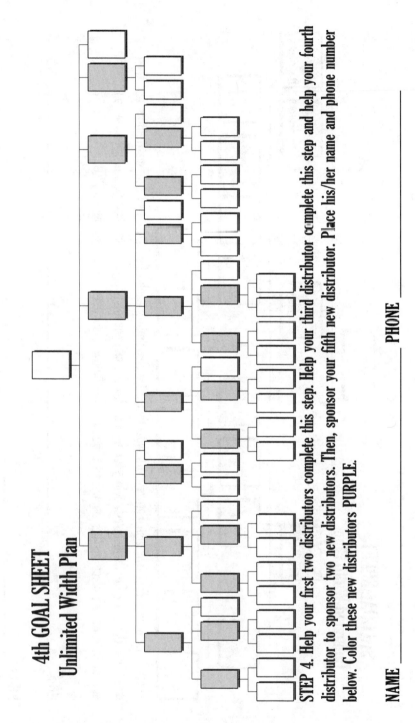

STEP 4. Help your first two distributors complete this step. Help your third distributor complete this step and help your fourth distributor to sponsor two new distributors. Then, sponsor your fifth new distributor. Place his/her name and phone number below. Color these new distributors PURPLE.

NAME _____   PHONE _____

The 1st Goal Sheet will have the distributor (JOHN) sponsor his first two distributors. History tells us that all distributors have the best opportunity to sponsor two people during their first week of a program. This is when their energy and excitement levels are highest; after all, they just paid their money for a distributor kit and starter products. With the help of their sponsor, they make two on one presentations and sponsor two new distributors. Without realizing it, John is being trained by his upline sponsor who is making the presentations. John has completed his first goal of sponsoring two distributors. Instruct John to color the two rectangles blue to signify that he has completed his first goal.

The 2nd Goal Sheet requires John and his sponsor to help John's two new distributors, to make presentations with them and help each sponsor two new distributors. John should also schedule appointments for himself and his sponsor to sponsor a third. When this goal sheet is completed, John will have three first generation distributors, and his first two distributors will have two each. His organization now contains seven distributors. He should color these rectangles yellow. Now, John not only has more training behind him, but he also has a graphic picture of his accomplishment. In many of the step plans, John would most likely have reached a pin level or advancement step in the marketing plan. John is just as proud of his completed goal sheets as he is of the commission check he earned, and he is being trained in a system that he will start training and teaching to others. John will have that natural enthusiasm in his voice when he starts training and teaching the system to others.

The 3rd Goal Sheet is a real turning point for John. He will make presentations with his first two distributors and their distributors' prospects to complete their individual goal sheets. When he colors these red, he will feel a new level of confidence because he was the one that made the presentations.

John will help his first two distributors with additional presentations so they will each sponsor a third new distributor. He will also make presentations with his third distributor to sponsor two new distributors and will feel a big boost of confidence when he colors all of these red.

John will still enlist the help of his sponsor to sponsor his fourth new distributor, but will make the presentation(s) with his sponsor looking on. John has now gained the knowledge and ability to prospect, sponsor, and train new distributors. He learned all of this from his sponsor and built his foundation using the step-by-step system in this book. John now has four first generation distributors, eight second level distributors, and eight third level distributors for a total of twenty distributors. His commission check is larger, and his downline sales organization is growing proportionally in width and depth. When he has colored all of these red, he will really feel that he has accomplished a lot, AND HE HAS!

The 4th Goal Sheet is the beginning of John's momentum stage, for this is where his organization will really start to grow. John will supervise his first two distributors, because they will be making presentations on their own with their distributors. John will sit in with them while they make presentations to sponsor their fourth new distributor. John will schedule presentation time for his third and fourth distributors, making presentations with them. John would now sponsor his fifth. He should ask his sponsor to sit in, but could have any of his distributors accompany him so he would not make the presentation by himself.

When John has completed his fourth goal sheet, he will be at the height of his confidence level with the company, the products, and himself. John is about to graduate into a real network marketer. He will now have developed an organization with five first generation distributors, thirteen second generation distributors, twenty third generation distributors, sixteen fourth generation distributors. His commission checks will reflect his new growth. When John looks at his Goal Sheet, his enthusiasm will skyrocket, and he will certainly pass this enthusiasm on to everyone he meets!

This system teaches a step-by-step proportional development system, teamwork, and true network marketing. John learned everything he knows about the business through being involved from the start. He actually helped to develop it and knows what to do, what to say, and where to place new distributors. John has graduated from network marketing's rookie school. His downline sales organization shows it graphically, and his commission check reflects his hard work and new skills. John is now ready to help everyone in his sales organization complete their goal sheets.

Unlike most other networkers that try to build downline sales organizations without an organized plan of action like this system, John is on his journey to success. Most networkers who do not work a plan of action like this system FAIL. There are far too many failures in this business simply because they do not have an organized plan of action.
In retrospect, John actually learned the business from participating

in it. In the beginning, he made a list of prospects and set appointments for his sponsor and himself to see each one. That is all John did. John accompanied his sponsor to these presentations and watched and listened. Repetition taught John what to say and do. The system structured his growth proportionately, and John developed a strong foundation that will provide him long-term residual income.

REMEMBER: "Don't Approach Without a Coach!" and "On the Phone NEVER Alone!"

Let these mottos be your guides in network marketing. They will be your strongest tools.

This system provides the following:

1   Goal Sheets
2   Training
3   Teamwork
4   Self-Esteem
5   Confidence
6   SUCCESS

Now, how important is your sponsor? A good sponsor is essential to the success of your program. Without a dedicated sponsor, you will have a high likelihood of failure; most people do. You must ask your sponsor for help. If you are refused, call your company immediately and ask to be reassigned to another sponsor in your area. This is your business, and you must go back to school in the beginning if you are going to be successful. Since your sponsor is your teacher, he/she must be willing to fulfill the true duties of a sponsor and follow the principles outlined in this system. The right sponsor may be difficult to find. You must have one that is willing to help you and one that knows the program.

The education you will gain from working with such a sponsor is the real benefit. You will learn to complete your first four goals and become a great sponsor yourself. This is your opportunity for success; do not let a bad sponsor take it away!

CHAPTER 8

THE BINARY MARKETING PLAN

The Binary Marketing Plan is a very viable distributor compensation program and certainly has merit. Unfortunately, there is a misconception borne by many network marketers that it is hard to work, and that one will always have a "runaway leg" that never pays. The traditional stair-step break-a-way and unilevel plans do indeed pay on all volume generated within a pay cycle or period. However, most binary plans do retain a certain amount of unpaid bonus volume. All one has to do is create matching volume to earn in these plans.

This book does not endorse or compare any marketing or distributor compensation plans. Rather, it serves as a blueprint on how to structure for maximum performance and teaches that people working with people make things happen.

There will continue to be a diversity of "improvements" to network marketing distributor compensation plans. This step-by-step system of building a network marketing downline is adaptable to all present plans and can be easily adapted to future improvements.

The same principles of our downline building system also apply to the binary marketing plan. The only difference is the placement of distributors in the structure and the relative compensation.

The four PRIMARY STEPS are reviewed below, and diagrams for the corresponding goal sheets are shown on subsequent pages.

STEP ONE - Sponsor your first two distributors. Place one LEFT and one RIGHT of your tracking center.

STEP TWO - Help them to sponsor their first two distributors and place each as you did - - one LEFT and one RIGHT. You now sponsor your third distributor and place on the LEFT OUTSIDE leg.

STEP THREE - Help your first two distributors to repeat the same process, sponsoring two new distributors each and placing them LEFT and RIGHT. They in turn should be helped to proceed in the same manner, sponsoring two new distributors each and placing them LEFT and RIGHT.. Next, work this same plan with your third new distributor. Then sponsor your fourth new distributor and place on the RIGHT INSIDE LEG.

STEP FOUR - Continue to support all of your distributors while they follow the building steps outlined above, and this is the time to help your fourth new distributor sponsor his/her first two distributors. You are now ready to sponsor your fifth new distributor and place on the OUTSIDE leg of the INSIDE of your LEFT leg.

Most networkers that work binary compensation plans have been under the misconception that by placing their personally sponsored people ONLY on the LEFT and RIGHT outside of their tracking number (business center), they are creating that magical carrot for their people to reach out for. This is true in part, but what about those who reside on the inside legs of their organization? By alternating to the inside of your tracking number and teaching this throughout your organization, you are creating MORE carrots. You will ultimately develop, by design, a stronger and much more profitable downline sales organization.

The binary system of compensation is just one form of distributor compensation derived from a certain structure. Once you understand the basics of a compensation plan structure, you will know that they are all capable of producing income. With this basic principle of sponsoring and placing structure, combined with working as a team in presenting the opportunity, you will be able to build an income with any company, no matter what structure its distributor compensation follows.

The key is to sponsor your first two distributors and help them sponsor their first two and then sponsor your third. By placing goal sheets in your distributors' hands, they will be able to follow in your footsteps while you all can share success together.

FIRST GOAL SHEET
Single Binary Tracking Center

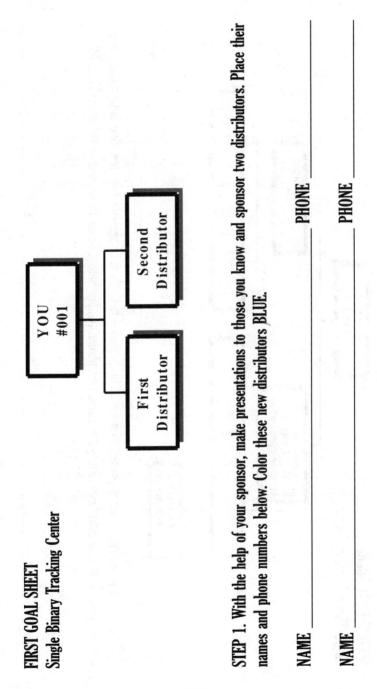

STEP 1. With the help of your sponsor, make presentations to those you know and sponsor two distributors. Place their names and phone numbers below. Color these new distributors BLUE.

NAME _____ PHONE _____

NAME _____ PHONE _____

SECOND GOAL SHEET
Single Binary Tracking Center

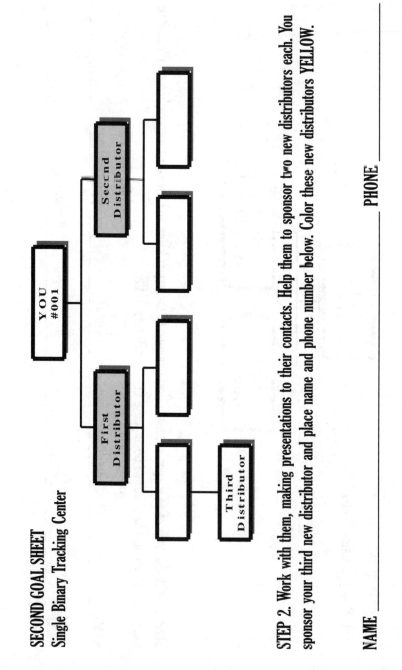

STEP 2. Work with them, making presentations to their contacts. Help them to sponsor two new distributors each. You sponsor your third new distributor and place name and phone number below. Color these new distributors YELLOW.

NAME _____   PHONE _____

THIRD GOAL SHEET
Single Binary Tracking Center

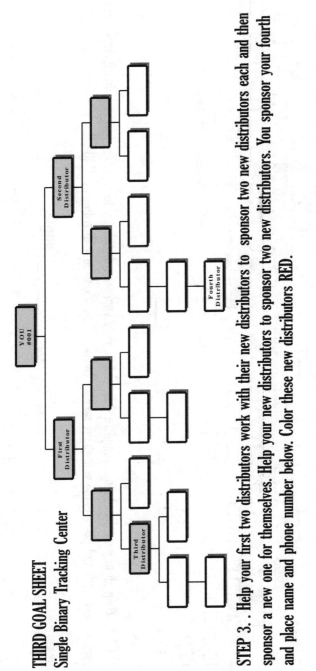

STEP 3. . Help your first two distributors work with their new distributors to sponsor two new distributors each and then sponsor a new one for themselves. Help your new distributors to sponsor two new distributors. You sponsor your fourth and place name and phone number below. Color these new distributors RED.

NAME _____ PHONE _____

FOURTH GOAL SHEET
Single Binary Tracking Center

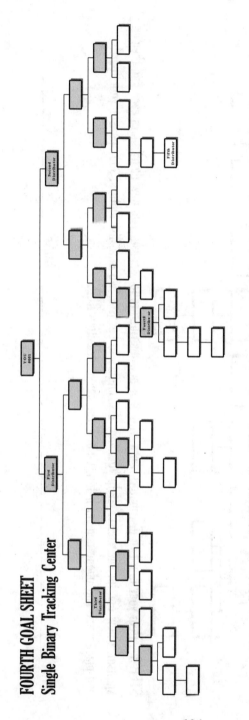

STEP 4. Help all of your distributors complete their charts. Help your new distributor to sponsor two new distributors. You sponsor your fifth and place name and phone number below. Color these new distributors PURPLE.

NAME _____   PHONE _____

THREE Tracking Number Binary Plans

If your company uses three income tracking numbers, known as "Tri-Packs," you will want to approach your building structure a little differently. Theoretically, if you build a Tri-Pack track-

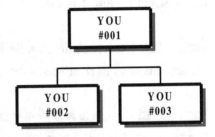

ing system, your first or primary center (#001) is directly above your second and third (#002, #003). By creating four legs (two below #002 and two under #003), you are in effect building three separate commission checks. Instead of building six legs to three separate tracking centers, you have to build only four because of the relationship of a tri-pack. Each of your secondary centers supports a different leg of your primary center. Therefore, as each secondary center builds left and right sales volume, your primary center accumulates the same volume.

Your first goal is to sponsor two new distributors. You will place one to the LEFT outside of your #002 center and one to the inside RIGHT of your #003 center.

Your second goal is to help these first two distributors each to sponsor two new distributors and duplicate your placement. You then sponsor your third new distributor and place this person to the RIGHT of your #002 center.

Your THIRD GOAL is to help your first two distributors complete their goal sheets and then help your third distributor to sponsor two new distributors. Next, sponsor your fourth new distributor. Place this person to the RIGHT of your #003 center.

You now have four legs started, and the volume will grow to produce commissions in all three of your tracking centers.

Your FOURTH GOAL is to help all of your distributors complete their goal sheets and to sponsor your fifth new distributor. Place this new distributor in the weakest leg you have.

As you continue to work with your distributors, helping them to grow with this system, you will continue to sponsor new distributors yourself. In the binary structure, you should place these personally sponsored representatives where they offer you the most benefit - - in your weakest position.

YOUR TRACKING CENTERS
Three Center BINARY

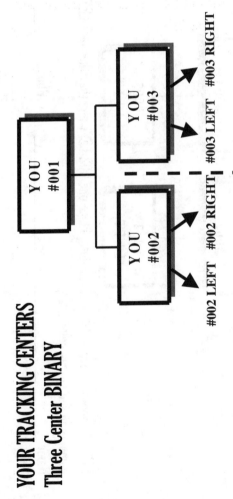

The above diagram is what your three tracking centers look like. You will be building a left and a right leg to #002 and #003. In STEP 1, you will build the LEFT of #002 and the LEFT of #003.

FIRST GOAL SHEET
Three Center BINARY

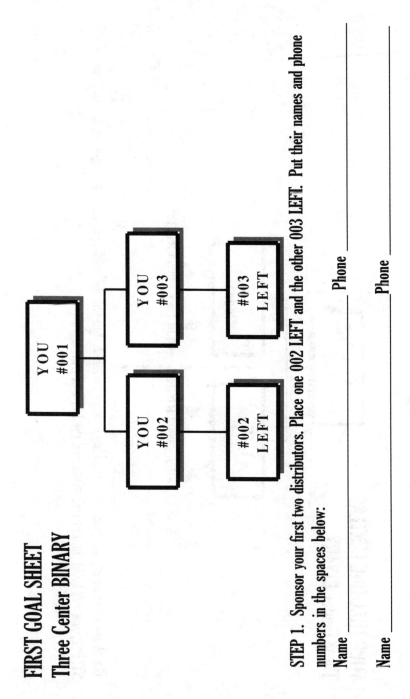

STEP 1. Sponsor your first two distributors. Place one 002 LEFT and the other 003 LEFT. Put their names and phone numbers in the spaces below:

Name _____ Phone _____

Name _____ Phone _____

SECOND GOAL SHEET
Three Center BINARY

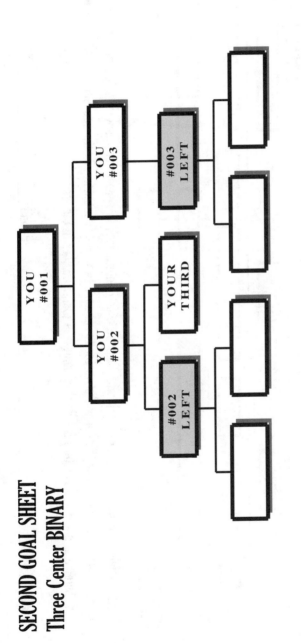

STEP 2. Help your first two distributors each to sponsor their first two distributors. Have them follow your placement in the FIRST GOAL STEP. You sponsor your third and place him/her 002 RIGHT. Put name and phone number in the space below:

Name _____ Phone _____

THIRD GOAL SHEET
Three Center BINARY

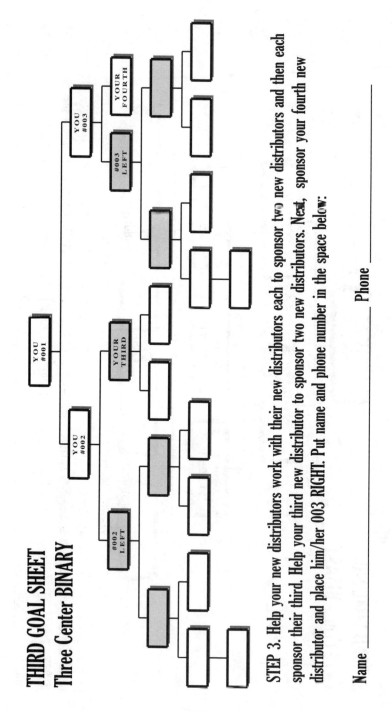

STEP 3. Help your new distributors work with their new distributors and then each sponsor their third. Help your third new distributor to sponsor two new distributors. Next, sponsor your fourth new distributor and place him/her 003 RIGHT. Put name and phone number in the space below:

Name _____   Phone _____

FOURTH GOAL SHEET
Three Center BINARY

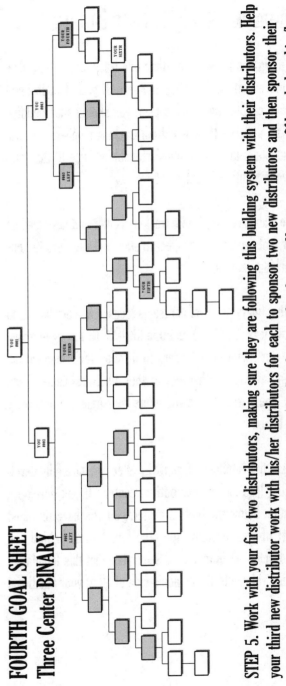

STEP 5. Work with your first two distributors, making sure they are following this building system with their distributors. Help your third new distributor work with his/her distributors for each to sponsor two new distributors and then sponsor their third. Help your fourth new distributor to sponsor his/her first two distributors. Next, sponsor your fifth and place him/her 002 LEFT. Put name and phone number in the space below:

Name _____   Phone _____

Linear or Straight-Line Binary

Some Binary programs having more than one tracking number allow straight line placements of tracking numbers. If you elect to build multiple tracking centers with such a plan, you should start building LEFT and RIGHT underneath your bottom tracking number. This will form the foundation and supply commissionable volume to the common side of your additional centers above.

Once you have stabilized the bottom tracking center and have leaders following your footsteps, you may elect to start building legs to your additional tracking centers.

The allure of the Binary plans, of course, is focused on your having to develop only two legs (One LEFT and One RIGHT). By having only two legs, you can work with your leaders to develop their momentum. When you start developing other legs to your additional centers, you are, in effect, "going wide." This will dilute your time and ultimately weaken your focus.

I recommend starting additional legs ONLY after you have fully developed your initial legs under your bottom center. If you develop a strong foundation below the bottom center, you will have the most important part of your organization (the foundation) behind you BEFORE you develop additional legs. Remember that this foundation will be supplying volume to the common side of all of your additional tracking centers.

The following illustration shows a group of four tracking centers. Instead of placing your additional tracking centers LEFT and RIGHT under your Primary tracking center (as in a Tri-Pack configuration), you will place them in a straight-line structure down the LEFT or the RIGHT side beneath each other. This is the reason it is called a LIN-EAR or STRAIGHT-LINE BINARY.

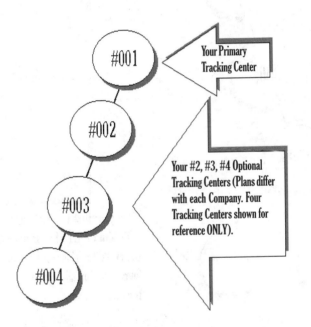

You will structure your first two distributors on the LEFT and RIGHT of the bottom tracking number (#004). Your third personally sponsored distributor will be placed off of your tracking center #003. Your fourth personally sponsored distributor will be placed off of your tracking center #002, and your fifth personally sponsored distributor will be placed off of your tracking center #001. These will all be structured either LEFT or RIGHT, depending on your LEFT or RIGHT relationship with your sponsor.

113

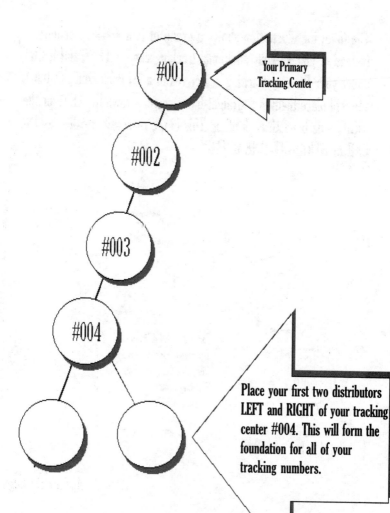

#001

Your Primary
Tracking Center

#002

#003

#004

Place your first two distributors
LEFT and RIGHT of your tracking
center #004. This will form the
foundation for all of your
tracking numbers.

With your sponsor's help, you sponsor two new distributors. Place
one to the LEFT and one to the RIGHT under your lowest tracking
number. Put their names and phone numbers below:

Name_____ Phone _____

Name_____ Phone _____

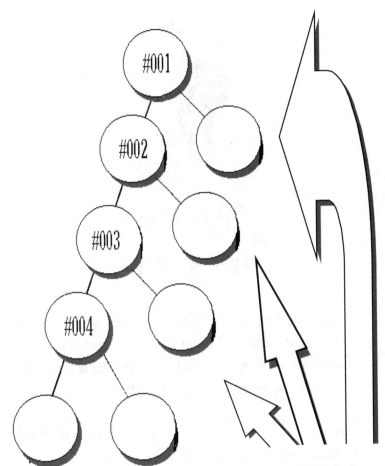

Additional Legs

You can build additional legs to #003, #002, and #001. As you develop these tracking centers, you will earn additional commission checks from each center.

NOTE: The volume produced from the LEFT and RIGHT Legs under #004 will be shared by #003, #002, and #001.

CHAPTER 9

SAMPLE ADVERTISING

The following are samples of "blind advertising" you can use to attract prospects. Most MLM companies will not object to your using blind advertising, since it does not mention the name of the company or the names or descriptions of the products.

Some of these ads use a double-line header in bold print. This is used to attract attention within the print media.

One of the most important aspects of advertising is to keep your ad in front of people each week. Running an ad once or twice will never produce the results you are looking for. You must advertise each week for an indefinite period of time.

You will be building your business from the new distributors you recruit through your advertising and with their WARM Market contacts. Therefore, your cost of advertising will be a minimal expense compared to the overall growth of your sales organization.

SAMPLE BLIND ADVERTISING

2nd Income Opportunity
Stay at home with your children and earn more money!
For appointment Call 222-2222

I'LL KISS YOUR WIFE
If you can't earn a second income with my
opportunity. Call 222-2222 for appointment

Start Today, Earn Today!
Full or Part-time Income Opportunity
For appointment call 222-2222

FIRE YOUR BOSS
Work from home and earn MORE Money!
For appointment 222-2222

JOB FOR SALE - CHEAP!
Own your own business! Unlimited Earning Potential.
Call for appointment. 222-2222

We Made It! 6 figure Income!
And we can help you too! Call for appointment. 222-2222

WANTED: Opportunity Seekers
Tremendous products, unlimited earning potential,
small investment. We provide complete training and help.
Call for appointment. 222-2222

RETIRE NOW
With the most awesome opportunity EVER! Complete
training and support! Call for appointment: 222-2222

MONEY, MONEY, MONEY
Unbelievable earning potential, Patented product line,
complete turnkey training. Small investment, 222-2222

WORK FOR YOURSELF, NOT BY YOURSELF
Call for appointment. 222-2222

The Secret to Wealth

Is something you have been doing ALL your life, but you never got paid. Let me show you how! Call for appointment. 222-2222

LOST $100,000

You will easily lose this much in the next twelve months unless you call today! Appointment only 222-2222

AWESOME PRODUCTS

Unlimited Income, just call me at 222-2222. We can help you open the door!

WORK FROM HOME

15 year old company expanding to this area. 222-2222!

CALL RAY TODAY

Tremendous Home Based Opportunity! Appointment Only 222-2222

HIRE YOUR BOSS

With the most awesome opportunity EVER! Complete
training and support! Call for appointment: 222-2222

INCOME OPPORTUNITY

No More Bosses, Unlimited Income Potential
We train and help you succeed.
For Appointment 222-2222

Hire Your Friends

Start your own business from home and let
them help! Complete training and help.
For appointment Call 222-2222

HIRE YOURSELF

Start your own business from home.
Complete training and help.
For appointment Call 222-2222

Unlimited Income Opportunity

Work from home with your children and earn more money!
For appointment Call 222-2222

WIN THE LOTTERY

Or join our success team. It is the Smart way to financial freedom! Call for appointment. 222-2222

OPPORTUNITY IS KNOCKING

We will help you open the door. Complete training and support. Call for appointment. 222-2222

SUCCESS FOR THE FEW

That join our team. Exciting FULL or part-time income! Call for appointment. 222-2222

Winners Will Call Immediately

Losers won't call at all! Tremendous opportunity for full or part-time income. Call for appointment. 222-2222

WANTED

Trainable, teachable, and highly motivated persons that want to earn MONEY. Call for appointment. 222-2222

Don't Rent, OWN Your Life!

With the most awesome opportunity EVER! Complete
training and support! Call for appointment: 222-2222

RIGHT PLACE, RIGHT TIME

The timing is perfect, the opportunity is awesome!
Call for appointment. 222-2222

Make Yourself Wealthy,

Not your Boss! Start your own full or part-time business
with this opportunity. 222-2222

Living Paycheck to Paycheck?

This opportunity could end that forever!
Call for appointment. 222-2222

The Secret to Wealth

Is something you have been doing ALL your life, but you
never got paid. Let me show you how! Call for appointment.
222-2222

You Are Already an Expert

At something you have been doing ALL your life, but you
never got paid. Let me show you how! Call for appointment.
222-2222

MONEY - MONEY - MONEY

Full or part-time income opportunity.
Call for appointment. 222-2222

If You Are Tired of Looking

For the Opportunity of your life, just call me at
222-2222. We can help you open the door!

For more information and tools please visit our Web Site at: www.mlmroadmap.com

Index

S

T

U

W

Application

The principles of structure outlined in this book can be adapted to any network marketing plan, regardless of configuration. If your plan is not illustrated, you can follow the "Unlimited Width" Goal Sheets as a blueprint for all network plans. The only difference will be in placement into your structure.

You can also contact the author through the website at www.mlmroadmap.com or write: Double Diamond Publishing, 7301 General Haig, New Orleans, LA 70124.

"All our dreams can come true . . . if we have the courage to pursue them."

Walt Disney

About the Author

Ray H. Duncan was Director of The Lajitas Museum and Desert Garden near the Big Bend National Park, where he also operated a Real Estate Office and was Editor and Publisher of "The Lajitas Sun" newspaper.

His interest in MLM began early when, as a youth, he was involved part-time with several network marketing programs. He became an avid student of the industry, and in 1990 started a full-time career which grew to include several corporate positions with network marketing firms.

Mr. Duncan formed his present consulting business in 1994, and his clients have ranged from start-up companies to established corporations seeking to improve their operations.